D-DAY

D-DAY

DUNCAN ANDERSON

SMITHMARK

This edition published in 1994
by SMITHMARK Publishers Inc.,
16 East 32nd Street,
New York, New York 10016.

SMITHMARK books are available for bulk purchase for sales promotion
and premium use. For details write or telephone the Manager of Special
Sales, SMITHMARK Publishers Inc., 16 East 32nd Street, New York, NY
10016. (212) 532-6600.

Produced by Brompton Books Corp.,
15 Sherwood Place,
Greenwich, CT 06830.

ISBN 0-8317-2190-1

Printed in Spain

10 9 8 7 6 5 4 3 2 1

PAGE 1: British infantrymen embark on an LSI in a preinvasion
exercise, May 1944.

PAGES 2-3: Preparing for D-Day. Equipment of the US 1st Infantry
Division is loaded onto the assault barges at anchor in the harbor
of an English south-coast port.

THESE PAGES: Having landed these troops on Utah Beach, LCVPs
return to their mother ships on the afternoon of 6 June.

CONTENTS

1

THE ATLANTIC WALL

Between 1942 and 1944 the Germans literally transformed the coast of France. The Atlantic Wall, a line of dense fortifications stretching from the Dutch-German frontier to Biarritz on the Franco-Spanish border, was modern Europe's largest-ever construction project. It took a quarter of a million conscripted laborers, 1.2 million tons of steel and over 15 million cubic meters of concrete to construct 15,000 permanent fortified positions. The Atlantic Wall, from design through to execution, was an exceptional feat by any standards. German defense-building on such a monolithic scale seems all the more extraordinary given that during the preceding three years the German Army had perfected the art of *Blitzkrieg*, a highly mobile form of armored warfare. The momentum of the German Panzer attack had mercilessly felled the virtually nonmechanized Polish Army, the fortification-obsessed French Army, and the heavily mechanized but incompetently commanded Soviet Army.

Why then, in early 1942, did the Germans throw all their resources into the building of static coastal defenses? The Russian Campaign had not gone as planned. The Wehrmacht had become bogged down only 31 kilometers from Moscow, and the Soviets had counterattacked on 5 December 1941. Two days later Japan, Germany's partner in the Axis Pact, attacked the American Pacific Fleet at Pearl Harbor; Hitler, constrained by the Pact, was forced to declare war on the United States on 11 December. From this time on an Anglo-American invasion of northwestern Europe became a real, if distant, possibility. In an ideal situation the German generals would have preferred to conduct their defense by concentrating Panzer divisions supported by fighter and bomber squadrons at strategic locations in the Low Countries and France. However, 80 percent of the German armor and much of the Luftwaffe's strength was being absorbed in attritional struggles with the Red Army and the RAF and USAAF. There were

ABOVE: From the summer of 1943 onward, B-17 bombers of the US Eighth Air Force, escorted by long-range Mustang and Thunderbolt fighters, began to dominate the air in the daylight hours over northwestern Europe. Split between the Anglo-American aerial onslaught in the west and the need to maintain control of the sky over the Eastern Front, the fighter forces of the Luftwaffe began to crumble.

RIGHT: The attrition of the Luftwaffe was accelerated by the destruction of many of Germany's refineries and synthetic oil plants. It was lack of fuel rather than lack of aircraft which finally brought the Luftwaffe to its knees.

LEFT: This photograph, taken by a French worker in May 1944, shows the Atlantic Wall at its strongest. A heavy gun placed in a massive concrete casement covers dense rows of obstacles.

ABOVE: The scene on the Dieppe beaches after the raid on 19 August 1942. A Canadian scout car lies bogged down in the shingle. Farther along the beach lie knocked-out tanks and grounded landing craft.

LEFT: The image of the Atlantic Wall presented in the German press. While it was true that the Pas de Calais and the Brittany ports were defended by heavy guns and sophisticated bunkers, the defenses of the rest of the French coast were at first much less formidable.

RIGHT: By the spring of 1942 large quantities of construction material were being required for the Atlantic Wall. Depots such as this sprang up all over northern and western France to sustain the largest-ever construction project in European history.

simply not enough tanks and aircraft available. In 1942 the Germans were therefore forced to resort to the defensive mode adopted by Hindenburg and Ludendorff in 1917, and by Maginot in the 1920s: the construction of a line of fortifications from which relatively low-grade infantry battalions would stand a good chance of inflicting heavy casualties on an attacker. Work began in earnest in March 1942; five months later the still-unfinished Dieppe defenses, manned initially by only 200 overage reservists, managed to defeat a landing attempt by 5000 Canadian and British troops.

Hitler saw the Dieppe victory as a vindication of the Atlantic Wall, perhaps even as a vindication of his own genius, since he had personally involved himself in the project. Hitler's World War I experience of horrendous artillery barrages, coupled with his architectural aspirations, equipped him, he felt, for the role of fortifications designer. He subsequently spent long hours drawing up plans with his Munitions Minister, Albert Speer. Speer later wrote in his memoirs that:

> 'Hitler planned these defensive installations down to the smallest details . . . Never sparing in self-praise, he often remarked that his designs ideally met all the requirements of a front-line soldier.'

Hitler might not have been the master architect he imagined, but he was certainly a capable military engineer, and the designs proved highly successful. The Atlantic Wall was composed of basically three types of position: the *Verteidigungsbereich*, a virtual fortress capable of protecting several battalions; the *Stützpunkt*, a position occupied by a unit from company up to battalion size; and the *Widerstandsnest*, which could hold a unit from section to platoon size. Some of these designs were to prove impenetrable to even the heaviest air attacks.

Clearly, air attacks would prove less successful if the German fortifications were invisible from both sea and air and if enemy aircraft were unable to locate their target. As the strength of the Luftwaffe ebbed away, the Germans became experts in camouflage. With Teutonic thoroughness they painted and shaded gun emplacements on cliffs until they merged with the surrounding rocks; the *Stützpunkt* pillboxes soon sported gabled roofs, windows and doors, making them indistinguishable from thousands of other French seaside buildings. The Germans also painted the sides of observation towers, which made them look from a distance just like typical Breton or Norman church steeples.

Most of Germany's munitions production was being absorbed by the fighting in Russia and later on the North-African and Italian fronts; there was therefore little artillery to spare for static fortifications. The Germans armed the Atlantic Wall with guns and heavy equipment stripped from the many defense lines they had previously overrun: the Czech Sudeten defenses, the Maginot Line and the Stalin Line. Concentrations were at their most dense at likely landing spots such as the Pas de Calais where there were 132 heavy guns in the 40-kilometer stretch between Calais and Boulogne. The Breton ports were also very heavily armed: the Germans needed to retain them in order to support their U-boat campaign; if they fell into enemy hands they would inevitably be used to sustain an Allied logistical build-up.

The Dieppe victory had revealed that British tanks were unable to climb a shale beach or a relatively small sea wall. German engineers now worked intensively to augment such natural difficulties with artificial obstacles. They transported wholesale to the French shores the entire Czech antitank defenses from the Sudetenland. These rows of tetrahedra — pyramids composed of five steel stakes — proved highly effective, and French foundries were soon being ordered to produce tens of thousands more. The Germans also implanted rows of curved rail obstacles with sharp ends farther down the beach, between three and five meters above the low-water mark. These were designed to rip the bottom out of any landing craft.

Minefields would further enhance the effectiveness of this already formidable barrier. Initially minelaying played a secondary role, but by spring 1944 the Germans were busy laying the largest minefield in history. By this time four million antitank and antipersonnel mines were already in place: eight times more than the previously largest field, laid

LEFT: In the spring of 1944, *Signal*, Germany's answer to *Life* magazine and *Picture Post*, carried many special features on the Atlantic Wall. The image of the heavy gun pointing seaward was designed to create a sense of security.

RIGHT: Hitler in the spring of 1944 looking rumpled and anxious. The German forces in Italy were holding their own, but the situation on the Eastern Front continued to deteriorate. Hitler believed that all would be well if his forces in the West could crush any invasion in the first few days. He would then be able to redeploy forces East.

BELOW: Lying atop a sand dune a German soldier mans an MG34 while a comrade scans the English Channel. In reality German machine guns were ensconced in formidable German pillboxes.

by the Soviets in the 12,950 square kilometer Kursk salient. These four million were but the first of a planned 220 million mines to be laid in two huge strips running across northern France; one strip 914 meters wide with a density of 10 mines per meter close to the coast and, farther inland, a second, deeper zone about 7315 meters across. Any invasion force attempting to penetrate the beaches would be in for a shock.

The Germans knew that the Allies would probably use massive airborne landings to supplement their coastal assaults. They correspondingly made all flat, clear areas which might be used for enemy paratroop and glider landings as hostile as possible, flooding low-lying areas drained by canals; in some areas water meadows became swamps, difficult but not impossible for heavily-laden airborne troops to negotiate. However, in the southeast of the Carentan peninsula the water was deep enough to drown paratroopers. In

drier regions German pioneers drove sharpened wooden stakes into fields and linked them with a latticework of wire so that they resembled gigantic bird nets. By the end of May, 5 million stakes were in place in northern France, and another 45 million were scheduled.

Ideally, the Wall's defensive properties would have been considerably enhanced by the German naval and air forces playing hob with the Allied convoys and assault formations, but the Navy's capacity was now reduced to little more than the occasional raid. By May 1944 Germany's naval commander in the west, Admiral Kranke, could boast only 40 U-boats, a flotilla of destroyers, and just 15 E-boats. His counterpart in the Luftwaffe, Marshal Sperrle, had initially been rather more optimistic. On 1 April Hitler had promised Air Fleet 3 (*Luftflotte 3*), the Luftwaffe forces in France, the speedy delivery of the first of 1000 new Messerschmitt Me

262 jet fighters, infinitely superior to any Allied airplanes. Two months later Sperrle was still waiting. In fact, by 1 June Air Fleet 3 had only 500 aircraft; of these, only 90 bombers and 70 fighters were operational. Despite this tiny capacity the Luftwaffe boasted 300,000 personnel in the west, of whom 100,000 were serving in the Luftwaffe's powerful III Flak Korps, a much more potent threat to enemy aircraft than the hapless fighter squadrons.

The defense of the west thus depended almost entirely on the Atlantic Wall and the men manning it. In the planning stage Hitler had thought 300,000 troops would be enough; however, the once-distant threat of invasion had by now become very real. In 1943 the Germans formed new coastal-defense divisions with men whose age or disabilities debarred them from the rapid-maneuver battles of the Eastern Front. The 70th Division, for example, consisted entirely of men suffering from stomach ulcers. Placed individually in other units, each would soon have become ill but, concentrated in their own division, special logistical arrangements could be made for acid-free rations. In late 1943 the so-called 'stomach divisions' were supplemented by divisions formed from volunteers from among the Soviet prisoners. The 276th Division boasted no fewer than eight different national groups, mainly from the Caucasus and central Asia, but also included a handful of confused Tibetans who had been press-ganged into the Soviet Army while grazing their herds near the Khazak border. The officers and NCOs of these divisions were often very good, reliable Wehrmacht veterans, whose capacity for rapid movement had been severely impaired by wounds and frostbite, but who understood the business of war and could be trusted to acquit themselves well in fighting from entrenched positions. In all, by May 1944, 34 such divisions had been formed and were positioned between Calais and Biarritz.

ABOVE: A 20mm antiaircraft gun and its Luftwaffe crew. The most formidable opposition the Allied aircraft faced was not from the Luftwaffe fighters but from thousands of antiaircraft guns like this.

BELOW: Turkomans captured by the Wehrmacht in the Caucasus now serving the Wehrmacht's 270th Division in Cherbourg receive instruction in beach defense.

ABOVE: Field Marshal Gerd von Rundstedt, appointed Commander in Chief West by Hitler, was responsible for overseeing the defenses of northwestern Europe before D-Day.

BELOW: Germany's most famous soldier, Field Marshal Erwin Rommel, inspecting bunkers in the Atlantic Wall late in 1943.

Fighting Among the Generals

Many senior Wehrmacht officers mistrusted static defenses, not least the commander of the German forces in the west, Field Marshal Gerd von Rundstedt. During an interview he gave for *Signal* magazine's special January 1944 feature on the Atlantic Wall, von Rundstedt let slip that 'we Germans do not indulge in the tired Maginot spirit.' Since arriving in France in March 1942 he had pressed hard for more mobile reserves. By early 1944 an additional 24 field divisions were in France, including 10 Panzer divisions, of which six were concentrated under General Leo Freiherr Geyr von Schweppenburg's command in forested areas to the north and northwest of Paris.

One very prominent German officer was not at all happy with this arrangement. In November 1943 Hitler had appointed Field Marshal Erwin Rommel to inspect the Atlantic Wall's defenses. Von Rundstedt quite rightly sensed that Rommel's roving commission posed a direct threat to his own position and he therefore attempted to undermine Rommel's authority by appointing him to a subordinate position. Rommel was to take command of the newly-formed Army Group B, responsible for the coastal area between the Dutch-German border and the Loire. Von Rundstedt assigned the remaining French coast and the frontier regions to Army Group G, under Field Marshal Blaskowitz. However, this arrangement created more problems than it solved. As Army Group B's commander, Rommel became increasingly critical of von Rundstedt's deployment of Panzer reserves. He asserted in one of his first reports to OKW that:

'With the coastline held thinly as it is at present the enemy will probably succeed in creating bridgeheads at several different points and in achieving a major penetration of our coastal defenses. Once this has happened, it will only be by the rapid intervention of our operational reserves that he

will be thrown back into the sea. *This requires that these forces should be held very close behind the coast defenses.'*

Rommel was effectively demanding control of Geyr von Schweppenburg's Panzer reserve. By March 1944 an unholy row was raging among the German generals. A series of crisis meetings, involving the Inspector General of Panzers, Heinz Guderian, and eventually Hitler himself, were concluded by a face-saving compromise which satisfied no one: the Panzer reserve would be placed under Hitler's direct control and would not be moved without his approval.

From the second week in March streams of Allied aircraft roared down on Army Group B's positions; British Lancasters and American B-17s pounded strong points from Belgium to the Gironde. Farther inland, medium and fighter-bombers set about the systematic destruction of the railroad system of northern France, reducing marshaling yards and railroad-repair shops to acres of twisted metal. All major bridges from Brussels to Toulouse were attacked and many destroyed. The antiaircraft gunners of III Flak exacted a fearful toll: by early June they had shot down nearly 2000 British and American aircraft and had killed some 12,000 Allied airmen. But still the aircraft came; indeed, the attacks intensified rather than diminished. The sheer scale of the aerial onslaught reinforced Rommel's fear that if the Allies ever got

ashore all would be lost. At one of the last conferences with Hitler before the invasion, Rommel's aide, Walter Spiedel, remembered that the Field Marshal had warned:

'If we are not at the throat of the enemy immediately he lands there will be no restoring the situation, in view of his vastly superior air forces. If we are not able to repulse the Allies at sea, or throw them off the mainland in the first 48 hours, then the invasion will have succeeded.'

The key to getting 'at the throat of the enemy immediately' lay in knowing the area in which he was likely to land. Von Rundstedt and the Wehrmacht intelligence apparatus still thought that to be the Pas de Calais. However, in March and April Rommel was clearly beginning to have doubts; a brilliant soldier, he almost intuitively began to divine the enemy's intention. An officer of the 1716th Artillery Regiment dug in at Ouistreham in Normandy, the seaport for Caen, recalled a dramatic moment during one of Rommel's tours of inspection in May 1944. Rommel called the officers together in a semicircle, but stood for a long time staring out to sea, ignoring them. He turned slowly and said 'Gentlemen, if they come they will come here.' In late May he set plans in motion for a considerable redeployment, ordering new units to Normandy and the Cotentin peninsula. Fortunately for the Allies, these moves had barely begun by the end of the first week of June.

ABOVE: The extra fuel provided by the drop tank attached to the belly of the Republic P-47 Thunderbolt allowed this formidable fighter to penetrate deep into German-controlled Europe and to engage in prolonged aerial combat with the Luftwaffe.

RIGHT: Bombs from B-17s scream down on a German airfield near Cognac on the French coast in the spring of 1944. Clouds of smoke billow up from the Luftwaffe's fuel depots.

2

THE ARMY OF THE SHADOWS

Despite fears about Allied air strikes, Rommel was reasonably confident that his forces would stand a fair chance of repelling a landing if deployed well forward in the Atlantic Wall's fortifications. His confidence would have evaporated had he realized that the Allies knew almost every detail of the Wall's construction, from the planning stages down to the last lick of paint. Ingenious camouflage may have hidden gun emplacements from aerial and naval reconnaissance, but it could not screen German construction work from the prying eyes of the French Resistance.

The first intelligence service to be set up in northern France after its collapse was the work of film-maker Gilbert Renault-Roulier. When France fell he had been making an epic about Christopher Columbus, due for release in 1942, the 450th anniversary of the discovery of the Americas – a motion picture which he hoped would bring him fame. However, by 1942 fame was the last thing Renault-Roulier wanted. In the two years which had elapsed he had escaped to London, had

joined de Gaulle's embryonic Free French forces, adopted the name Colonel Rémy, and had returned to northern France to organize resistance. By the spring he had established the beginnings of an intelligence network, the Confrérie Notre-Dame, which would cover the entire northern coast within the year. In May 1942 one of Rémy's first agents, René Duchez, a house painter in Caen, carried off an astounding intelligence coup. Hired by the Todt Organization to paint its offices in Caen, the short, nondescript Duchez was simply part of the scenery for the German draftsmen working on plans of the defenses; so much so that when a 6-meter square blueprint of part of the Atlantic Wall disappeared, no one suspected Duchez. Within days Rémy had personally smuggled this prize across the English Channel in a fishing boat, and was unfolding it in de Gaulle's office in London.

Rémy's steal set the pattern for the next two years, during which thousands of sketches and photographs of the construction work, from Calais to Biarritz, were smuggled to

ABOVE RIGHT: By spring 1944 the Resistance was becoming increasingly effective as a conventional military force. Anglo-French SOE teams parachuted into France to train the eager but often unskilled *Maquis*.

RIGHT: The Resistance fighters in Brittany were particularly well armed and knew how to take care of their weapons. Early in 1944 a Breton Resistance group carried out a daring raid on a German HQ in St Malo, which netted a vital report on defenses in the Atlantic Wall.

LEFT: The popular image of the French Resistance. Although the Resistance was to prove invaluable in disrupting German lines in the summer of 1944, its most invaluable work in 1942 and 1943 lay in gathering intelligence.

LEFT: Throughout 1942 and 1943, the parachute drop, often unreliable and dangerous, was the main way of getting men and materiel to the Resistance. By early 1944 Lysander liaison aircraft had made the process almost routine.

BELOW LEFT: The *Milice*, a right-wing French collaborationist paramilitary force, round up Resistance suspects. For much of the occupation the *Milice* posed a far greater threat to the Resistance than did the Germans.

RIGHT: A member of the Resistance taps out a coded message from his HQ to London. By the spring of 1944 about 150 such radios were in operation in northern France.

BELOW RIGHT: The Free French intelligence service in London was large and sophisticated by 1944. Here messages are being decoded before being passed on to the relevant departments within SHAEF.

England. However, few Resistance members had Duchez's luck. As the Germans grew more security-conscious they stepped up Gestapo raids, to which the Resistance retaliated by developing increasingly ingenious techniques. One of Colonel Rémy's men, posing as a real-estate agent, toured the coastal towns of Normandy and Brittany openly photographing 'desirable seaside residences with panoramic views.' His brochures were eagerly perused in London. Some Norman and Breton fishermen proved very adept at gathering information. The fishermen noticed that whenever the Germans installed a new coastal gun they scheduled a practice shoot out over the English Channel, heralding each exercise with a warning to fishermen to clear the area. Using their detailed knowledge of the coastline, the fishermen were able to map virtually every German gun emplacement. Maurice Dounin, an art teacher at Caen's lycée, turned information-gathering into an art form. For months Dounin bicycled and walked up and down the Norman coast, sketching every German fortification and taking copious notes. His portfolio was then converted into a detailed 15-meter map of the area from the mouth of the Dives to the Cotentin peninsula, which soon found its way to London.

Photographs and sketches were invaluable but took time to collect. Early in 1944 a Resistance group in Brittany took direct action, with a daring raid on the German headquarters at St Malo. At the bottom of the sack of documents which they managed to carry off they found the report of a recent inspection carried out by Rommel, complaining that 'in one section, several hundred kilometers wide, only a handful of mines have been installed.' Such information proved of particular interest to London.

By spring 1944 the French Resistance was yielding a flood of information. In northern France alone it was operating 150 radios; in just one month these had transmitted 700 detailed reports to London. During the same period 3000 written dispatches were sent to London, mainly through couriers using the now almost regular nightly cross-Channel Lysander liaison aircraft. These messages went first to Colonel Rémy, now the head of an increasingly large Free French intelligence service, where they were analyzed and then forwarded to the appropriate departments within SHAEF.

The French paid a terrible price for the invaluable information they handed on to the Allied high command. By spring 1944 the almost lax atmosphere in northern France of only two years earlier had changed to one of near-hysterical suspicion. The Gestapo patrolled likely invasion sites with draconian rigor, arresting and interrogating thousands of subjects before dispatching them to concentration camps. Many of the bravest and most resourceful Resistance members, including Maurice Dounin, were placed before firing squads and executed.

3

THE GENESIS OF D-DAY

When the Germans began constructing the Atlantic Wall in spring 1942, an Allied amphibious assault on the French coast seemed only a remote possibility. Had Hitler but known it, Churchill himself was opposed to the idea. In 1915 the fiasco of the British and Dominion landing at Gallipoli, in which 250,000 men were killed or wounded, had come close to destroying Churchill's political career. British leaders were still haunted by memories of all the losses incurred by the various frontal assaults against prepared positions of World War I. Consequently, under Churchill's direction the British now pursued an indirect wartime strategy as Germany's power made direct action impossible for the time being. British leaders developed a strategy of opposition in peripheral theaters, where the strength of the Royal Navy would give British forces the advantage. At the very time when Germany began to construct the Atlantic Wall, Britain was more concerned with holding Egypt and defeating Axis forces in North Africa.

Hitler and Mussolini's declaration of war on 11 December 1941 brought the United States into the European conflict. The American population had mixed feelings about entering the war: most demanded the defeat of Japan after the attack on Pearl Harbor but felt less happy about US involvement in Europe, not simply because a high proportion of the American population was of German or Italian origin. It was genuinely suspected that Britain would use US power largely to further its own ends. The State Department and the Joint Chiefs of Staff had no desire to see America bankroll British schemes for what seemed like imperial aggrandizement in the Mediterranean, schemes which would not bring the war to an end. The Americans believed that a speedy conclusion to the war could only come one way: by landing in northwest Europe, creating a second front, and driving on Germany.

This was the argument which Roosevelt's aide, Harry Hopkins, and US Chief of Staff, General Marshall, carried with them to London on 8 April 1942. They also took the first detailed plans for an invasion, drawn up by the recently promoted Major General Dwight D Eisenhower. Only three years earlier Eisenhower had been serving as a major in the Philippines under General Douglas MacArthur. In late 1939 Eisenhower had managed to secure himself a transfer to the War Plans Department in Washington. Here his personal advice on stratagems for handling the difficult and imperious MacArthur had proved invaluable to Marshall and Roosevelt. Eisenhower achieved rapid promotion. He was a good staff officer but knew nothing about amphibious operations. Nor, for that matter, did anyone else in the American military establishment; American forces had made their last landing in 1898 against weak opposition during the Spanish-American War.

Operations Sledgehammer and Round Up

Like most American schemes in early 1942, Eisenhower's plans for the landing were overly optimistic and half-baked. He argued that the Western Allies had to be ready to land forces if a collapse of Soviet resistance seemed imminent. At this stage the Americans had few forces in Britain, and one plan, Operation Sledgehammer, required the British to sacrifice between eight and 10 divisions. Eisenhower's other plan, Operation Round Up, was marginally more sound. By 1 April 1943 he wanted to be able to land six British and American divisions on the French coast somewhere between Boulogne and Le Havre. Reinforcements would follow at the rate of 100,000 men a week until a force of 30 American and 18 British divisions was in Europe. The invasion would require 7000 landing craft (yet to be built), 3300 American and 2500 British aircraft, few of which had yet left the factory.

Dieppe

The British Chiefs of Staff paid lip service to Round Up but were extremely dubious about both plans. The fate which met Operation Jubilee, the Anglo-Canadian raid on Dieppe, soon turned their doubts into hostility. In the early hours of 19 August 1942 a joint force – 5000 Canadians, 1100 British commandos and 50 American rangers – went ashore at Dieppe. The highly-trained, experienced commandos tasked with attacking German coastal defense guns to the east and west of Dieppe conducted a successful operation. The flamboyant Lieutenant Colonel Lord Lovat led No. 4 Commando in a ferocious attack against the battery at Berneval, six kilometers east of Dieppe, and virtually wiped out the German defenders. Meanwhile, No. 3 Commando, reduced to one landing craft and 20 men after a battle in the English Channel with German E-boats, put ashore at the Varengeville battery, six kilometers to the west of the town. Major Peter Young, the surviving senior officer, led his small command into a furious assault which pinned down the German gunners for the next three hours.

With the flanking defense batteries out of action, the bulk of the Canadians came ashore at Dieppe. Since the town was defended by only 200 overage reservists, the attack should have been a foregone conclusion, but it turned into a disaster. The firing to the east and west alerted the Germans who immediately occupied strong positions, setting up their machine guns in newly-constructed cliffside pillboxes and in the upper rooms of houses with a clear view of the beach. The handful of Germans poured a stream of fire into the landing craft, cutting swathes through the Canadians as they struggled out of the water.

With the Canadians held on the beach the Germans rushed reserves to Dieppe. The result was a massacre. By late afternoon von Rundstedt could report to his Führer the satisfying news that 'no armed Englishman remains on the continent.' The British and Canadians left behind 3648 dead and wounded men and prisoners at Dieppe. Some 500 of those who made it back to England were very badly wounded, whereas the Germans took comparatively few casualties. The assault had gone disastrously wrong. There was no co-ordination between air, sea and land forces, and when air and naval gunfire support finally arrived it proved woefully inadequate. Worse still, the Allies' Churchill tanks had handled the beach conditions very badly – they either dug into the shale or shed tracks when trying to climb the sea wall.

The Creation of COSSAC

However, the triumphant German victory at Dieppe proved Pyrrhic. The Americans, shocked out of their naïve optimism about the ease with which major amphibious operations could be conducted, entered Allied invasion discussions in a newly-somber mood. They now saw that meticulous advance planning was vital for a full-scale invasion, thereby leaving absolutely nothing to chance. First, they needed to establish a professional planning staff. In January 1943 Roosevelt, Churchill and the Combined Chiefs of Staff met at Casablanca. Here they demanded the unconditional surrender of the Axis powers, and agreed to press ahead with Operation Round Up.

Eight weeks later, the British logistics specialist Lieutenant General Sir Frederick Morgan was appointed Chief of Staff to the Supreme Allied Commander (COSSAC), with the job of planning the invasion. Morgan's offices in Norfolk House in London's St James's Square were soon filled with the best staff which the British and US Armies could provide. Their numbers were then swelled by transfers from Lord Louis Mountbatten's Combined Operations Headquarters, the organization which had planned many commando raids.

The size of Morgan's planning staff was unprecedented, and so too was the complexity of the operation it was to plan. Two months later Morgan learned that Churchill and Roosevelt, meeting at the Trident Conference in Washington, had decided that the landings should take place on 1 May 1944 – codenamed 'D-Day'. Fully aware of the operation's portentous historical significance, they replaced the American codename 'Round Up' with the codename 'Overlord', a name resonant with implications of heroism and victory.

The Decision for Normandy

Dieppe had taught the Allies that they could not hope to take even a weakly-defended port without suffering unacceptable casualties. Consequently, the landings would have to take place on open beaches well away from fortified harbors. The Pas de Calais had many advantages. It offered the shortest route across the English Channel: the navy could land more men and materiel in less time than elsewhere. The Allied air forces favored it for similar reasons, as short distances cut down the need for refueling, so they could keep their fighters in the air longer and provide increased protection for an invasion fleet. The armies welcomed the direct route which the Pas de Calais offered to Germany's industrial heartland, the Ruhr, a route which reduced the logistical difficulties of sustaining rapidly-advancing forces.

However, the disadvantages were overwhelming. The Pas de Calais was cursed with high cliffs and narrow shingle beaches, which posed enormous problems for heavy tracked vehicles. Natural difficulties, coupled with an intense level of German defense, meant that a major landing on the Pas de Calais might be like Dieppe multiplied by a factor of 30.

One largely American group in COSSAC argued hard instead for a Brittany landing. Brittany's long, heavily-indented coastline with a number of good beaches offered obvious advantages. A successful landing might also lead to the cap-

TOP: General Dwight D Eisenhower, appointed to command the Allied invasion forces on 7 December 1943. Eisenhower's rise had been meteoric. Just four years earlier he had been serving as a much-abused aide to General Douglas MacArthur in the Philippines.

ABOVE: Some of the survivors of the Dieppe raid disembark at Newhaven. Although the raid had been disastrous, commandos and a detachment of US troops (seen here) scored notable successes during the assault.

ture of one of Brittany's large ports from the landward side; but the great distance between Brittany and Germany would enormously increase Allied logistical difficulties. It was also really too far from England for Allied fighter aircraft to provide constant and effective air cover and support. In addition, the beaches of Brittany were exposed to the southwest winds of the Atlantic. The storms on this coast were savage and unpredictable and the coast itself was studded with potentially dangerous islets and reefs. Royal Navy officers attached to COSSAC were horrified by the prospect of a Brittany landing. They persisted in reminding their American colleagues of the numerous disasters suffered along this stretch of coast by both the British and French fleets in previous centuries.

That left only two stretches of the Atlantic and Channel coasts: from the Gironde to the Spanish border (too far away), and from the estuary of the Seine to the Cotentin peninsula, the coast of Normandy. The Normandy coast featured long, wide sandy beaches backed by dunes and low cliffs. It presented none of the difficulties of the Pas de Calais or Brittany. Moreover, the Cotentin peninsula, jutting north into the Channel, protected the beaches from the storms that almost invariably came in from the southwest. The beaches were also midway between two heavily-defended major ports, Le Havre and Cherbourg. Once ashore, Allied armies would have the option of capturing either or both from the landward side. All the arguments were weighed up and assessed at the Rattle Conference convened by Mountbatten's Combined Operations Headquarters in Scotland on 28 June 1943. Normandy emerged as the only real possible landing site.

Mapping the Coast

Once the landing site had been decided upon, COSSAC stepped up its intelligence gathering. The invaluable information already collected by the French Resistance had been forwarded to the Inter-Services Topographical Unit based in Oxford. In offices along St Giles a staff made up of geography dons and Royal Navy officers recorded and sifted every piece of information: the composition of the beaches, the nature of the currents, and the times of the tides. This was all incorporated in a minutely-detailed scale model of the Normandy coast being built in the basement of the city's Ashmolean Museum. Lieutenant Commander J E Taylor remembered feeling a strange sense of awe when he first walked into the Ashmolean model room, COSSAC's inner sanctum:

'That was the secret place of secret things that were laid out on tables – one much larger than the others dominating the room. I moved toward it and from where I stood a glass sea, shaded through dark blue, light blue, and pale green, stretched toward a miniature coastline. There was a thin film of dust upon that motionless sea which proved there was no routine invasion of charwomen with buckets, brooms and mops into that room. The model did not proclaim the locality of the section of coastline it represented. Only someone who knew it intimately would recognize it, but I knew that I was looking at a scale model of the Normandy beaches. It looked so pleasingly toy-like with its colored sea, sandy beaches, miniature houses and green fields beyond, that it seemed to have no connection with the battleground.'

The Inter-Services Topographical Unit insisted that facts be checked again and again. To supplement the work of the Resistance, reconnaissance aircraft took millions of high- and low-level photographs, while motorboats and miniature submarines took swimmers to within a few hundred meters of the shore. From here they swam onto the beaches to test the composition of the sand with augers. On the basis of the Ashmolean model, the Topographical Unit was able to prepare accurate and detailed maps of enemy-occupied territory. In all, 170 million individual maps were printed, of which 40,000 were top-secret maps of the invasion beaches, detailing the German defenses right down to barbed-wire entanglements and tetrahedra.

Landing Craft

Deciding where to land was only one of the problems COSSAC had to solve. The Dieppe raid had shown that landing large forces was fraught with danger. The Canadians and commandos had gone ashore in wooden craft with lightly-armored sides which relied on speed and maneuverability to protect the men. In large-scale operations it was essential that the craft sail at a constant speed and on rigidly-determined routes, otherwise chaos would ensue. New steel boats, the Landing Craft Assault (LCA), were designed which could be carried aboard troop transports and lowered from davits.

LEFT: Churchill tanks disembark from one of the new Landing Craft Tanks (LCTs) during a training exercise on the southwest coast.

Armored support would come ashore in Landing Craft Tank (LCT) barges, which could carry from three to five tanks, and Landing Ship Tanks (LSTs), huge ocean-going shallow-bottomed ships which could ground themselves on gently sloping beaches and disgorge as many as 60 tanks.

The disaster at Dieppe had shown how vital it was that assault forces going to the beaches be reinforced by fire support. The Royal Navy solved the problem by fitting LCTs with banks of five-inch rockets. A single LCT could fire 1080 rockets in just 30 seconds, more than the combined firepower of all the cruisers of the Royal Navy firing simultaneously. Three dozen LCTs were fitted out in this manner, giving the landing forces immense firepower.

The 'Funnies'

Dieppe reinforced yet another lesson, one first learned on the Somme in World War I: infantry could only advance against entrenched machine-gunners when supported by armor. COSSAC planners therefore insisted that tanks should spearhead the Normandy assault. In March 1943 the Chief of the Imperial General Staff, General Alan Brooke, ordered the formation of the 79th Armoured Division, and placed in command one of the great pioneers of armored warfare, Major General Percy Hobart. Within weeks Hobart had assembled around him some of Britain's finest engineers, who applied themselves enthusiastically to the task in hand: to design and build vehicles which could negotiate German obstacles.

They came up with an extraordinary variety of machines ('Funnies'). The most conventional was the 'DD' (Duplex Drive) or swimming tank, a Sherman fitted with propellers driven by its main engine and a canvas skirt to give it buoyancy. These tanks would land either before or with the infantry. Minefields were to be destroyed by 'Crabs,' tanks fitted with rotary drums which flailed the ground with steel chains. The strongest German blockhouses were to be literally cracked open by the 'Petard', the Armoured Vehicle Royal Engineers (AVRE Mk III), equipped with a huge mortar capable of hurling an explosive charge the size of a garbage can. Once the reinforced concrete was cracked, Mark VII Crocodile tanks equipped with flamethrowers would shoot in high-pressure jets of liquid fire. It was a formidable array: the modern equivalent of medieval siege engines. To help them negotiate ditches and walls, Churchill tanks were fitted with box-girder bridges.

ABOVE: LCTs were fitted with banks of five-inch rockets. These formidable vessels could give troops ashore immense fire support, something which had been lacking at Dieppe.

BELOW: The first experiments with 'swimming tanks': Valentines with inflatable canvas skirts prepare to 'swim' ashore off Moray Firth in Scotland.

Artificial Harbors

Even if the new landing craft and siege engines got the troops ashore, how could sizable forces be sustained over open beaches? COSSAC's most optimistic assessments estimated a two-week period between the first landings and the capture of Cherbourg, and a further two to three months to clear the mines and repair the damage left by the Germans. In fact Churchill had come up with the solution 25 years earlier, when the British had been preparing to break the Western Front deadlock by landing behind German lines on the Flemish coast. He had suggested building 'a number of flat-bottomed barges or caissons, made not of steel but of concrete, which would float when empty of water and thus could be towed across. On arrival the seacocks would be opened and the caissons would settle on the bottom. By this means a torpedo- and weather-proof harbor would be created in the open sea.' The COSSAC naval commander, Admiral John Hughes Hallet, incorporated Churchill's idea in his construction plans for two artificial harbors, later codenamed 'Mulberry A' and 'Mulberry B'. Mulberry A, designed to supply the Americans, was to be towed to the east of Pointe du Hoe, while Mulberry B, to support the British, was to be towed into

position off Arromanches 15 kilometers to the east. This operation alone would require 150 very powerful tugboats. To protect the harbors, COSSAC planned two great artificial reefs, made by sinking some 74 old cargo vessels and obsolete warships. When in position, the two harbors would be able to unload 12,000 tons of stores and 2500 vehicles a day. Before production began, Hughes Hallet ordered scale replicas of the Mulberries to be inserted into the model in the Ashmolean's basement. Lieutenant Commander Taylor, the officer tasked with selecting the blockships, was one of the first to see the completed model. He later recorded his astonishment:

'It represented perfection. This was the completed harbor as designers designed it, planners planned it, and the unwritten orders confidently ordained that it should take place. Cargo ships that had arrived lay at anchor discharging. The blockships were so sunk in orderly line with the breakwater so formed, extended by addition of Phoenix to the eastward and westward and round to the shore.

The real Phoenix were concrete caissons in sizes that ranged from 200 to 6000 tons, but in that model they appeared as only tiny oblongs of wood. Within the harbors' breakwaters the floating roadways stretched from the shore toward the spud pierheads, where miniature coasters, with derricks topped, lay alongside. It was relatively simple to put such things on paper and build such models to present in pictorial form all that the papers intended, but was there any possibility of such perfect achievement in reality?'

The Mulberry harbor project was a vast undertaking – in construction terms, the British equivalent of the German Atlantic Wall. In October 1943 orders were placed with shipyards from the Clyde to the Tyne. The yards were to construct more than 200 steel and concrete caissons, some as much as 60 meters long, 18 meters high, and weighing 6000 tons. There were also to be floating pierheads, 16 kilometers of steel roadway, and 93 steel and concrete floats each weighing 2000 tons. As soon as the yards launched the component parts, they were to be sunk immediately in the Tyne, the Clyde and a hundred other rivers, estuaries, and sea lochs. Here they could be hidden from German reconnaissance until needed, when the water would be pumped out and the Phoenix caissons would re-emerge from the depths.

Operation Bolero

As COSSAC labored to perfect the invasion plans, the face of Britain was being transformed. During Operation Bolero, the codename for the American build-up, US Army forces in Britain grew from 36,000 in May 1942 to 1.5 million by May 1944. The American flow of materiel for the invasion was even more striking: in the 24 months between April 1942 and April 1944, five million tons of military freight flowed through British ports, 10 percent of the total tonnage of all goods imported into Britain during this time. This seemed an enormous allocation to British port officials, but it was not nearly enough. In the early months of 1944 a mountainous backlog of cargo piled up in New York, threatening to delay the invasion. Churchill intervened directly, ordering that imports for civilian consumption be cut further – thereby imposing increasingly severe rationing on an already exhausted population. By the end of May the Americans had moved to England 50,000 tanks and armored vehicles, 450,000 trucks and 450,000 tons of ammunition, transforming the country, in Eisenhower's words, into 'the greatest operating military base of all time.'

Other military build-ups were also underway. By May 1944 the Canadian Army had sent nearly 200,000 troops to Britain; the Poles and Free French together fielded 40,000, and the Belgians, Dutch, Norwegians and Czechs accounted for perhaps another 10,000. But the largest army, at least initially, was the British: by spring 1944 it stood at 1.75 million within the British Isles. All told, the Allies had three million men waiting in southern England, while another one million Americans would come directly from the USA, and nearly 100,000 Canadians would arrive both from Canada and from the Canadian forces in Italy.

The Creation of SHAEF

Until late 1943 Churchill had assumed that a British general would command the invasion forces. He had already half-promised the job to his faithful CIGS, General Alan Brooke, but the Americans had other ideas. Given the preponderance of US troops, an American commander seemed a more logical choice. Roosevelt prevaricated until 7 December 1943 and then appointed General Eisenhower, a choice that surprised many. Eisenhower was a first-rate administrator and staff officer, responsible for the Round Up plan, but only four

LEFT: A small part of the Mulberry harbor: three 2000-ton concrete floats, each larger than a heavy destroyer, under construction in the London docks.

BELOW: Some of the 1.5 million American troops in Britain by May 1944. To the left are reminders of the operation on which they would soon embark: waterproofed jeeps and camouflaged half-tracks.

ABOVE: American M4 Shermans, silhouetted against the Bristol Channel, roll up a ridge toward Exmoor for an armored exercise. The high silhouette of the Sherman proved to be a major disadvantage because German antitank gunners found it made an easy target.

LEFT: When he was not in his office at Bushey Park, Eisenhower spent as much time as possible visiting units in training. Here the Supreme Commander talks to paratroopers of the 82nd Airborne Division.

RIGHT: The crew of a Sherman tank, relaxing after an exercise on Dartmoor, enjoy the panoramic view. Training in this terrain proved of limited value because conditions in Normandy were very different.

years earlier he had been a lowly major and had never commanded large forces in action. On his arrival in Britain in January 1944, Eisenhower established the Supreme Headquarters Allied Expeditionary Force (SHAEF) in Bushey Park by the Thames. This HQ assimilated the COSSAC staff; by spring, SHAEF was home to some 7000 personnel.

In the meantime, Eisenhower had been busy constructing a team of subordinate commanders. The deputy he chose was British, but not a general: Air Chief Marshal Arthur Tedder, former Commander in Chief of Allied air forces in the Mediterranean. Tedder was a firm advocate of air, land and sea co-operation; quite unlike many airmen, who seemed convinced that their bomber fleets could win the war by themselves. Tedder's views were shared by Air Chief Marshal Trafford Leigh-Mallory, who took command of the new Allied Tactical Air Force, formed from the RAF's Second and the USAAF's Ninth Tactical Air Forces. Naval forces would obviously play a vital role, and Eisenhower agreed to Churchill's suggestion of Admiral Bertram Ramsay for the commanding post. Ramsay's skill, both at getting forces ashore and back to sea was unmatched: he had commanded both the Dunkirk evacuation in 1940 and the Allied landings in North Africa in November 1942. Churchill may have pressed for Ramsay's appointment with the unspoken thought that were things to go badly wrong on D-Day, he would be an ideal admiral to take control. It was harder to choose a general to command the ground forces. In North Africa Eisenhower had been very impressed by General Harold Alexander, a former officer of the Irish Guards. Alexander, impeccably dressed, ramrod straight and stiff upper-lipped, looked just like the Hollywood stereotype of a British general, but many of his British colleagues had a much lower

opinion of his abilities. The CIGS General Alan Brooke pushed hard to appoint Britain's most successful general, the egotistical and acerbic General Bernard Montgomery. Eisenhower accepted Montgomery's appointment with deep misgivings, but had no such doubts about appointing Lieutenant General Omar Bradley to command the US First Army. Bradley, an old and close friend, was Montgomery's very antithesis.

This team probably represented the best possible from the senior commanders available in early 1944. Eisenhower proved himself an excellent 'chairman of the board.' Having served as executive officer to General Douglas MacArthur, he was used to dealing with prima donnas and egocentrics. On many occasions over the next few months Eisenhower's tact and charm kept the complicated human machinery of SHAEF working. Montgomery, who secretly despised Eisenhower, constantly patronized him; Eisenhower may have vented his frustrations in private, but never in public.

The Transportation Plan

Early in 1944, one of Eisenhower's chief tasks was ensuring a smooth working co-operation between the Allied forces and their land, sea and air components. The armies and the navies worked together relatively harmoniously; but not the Allied air forces. Since 1942 Air Chief Marshal Arthur Harris's Bomber Command and US General Carl Spaatz's Eighth Air Force had waged a massive air offensive against Germany. Both men had boasted that, given 30 days of uninterrupted bombing, they could win the war by themselves. Back in SHAEF, Tedder and Leigh-Mallory had formulated a transportation plan which demanded the concentration of the RAF and USAAF's entire resources on disrupting and destroying northern and western France's communication

LEFT: The Supreme Commander shoots a disapproving glance at his Chief of Staff, Lieutenant General Walter Bedell Smith and Air Chief Marshal Sir Trafford Leigh-Mallory, whose exchanges have interrupted a press photo opportunity. The photograph, taken on 12 February 1944 at Bushey Park, shows the entire command team. These are, left to right: Lieutenant General Omar N Bradley, Commander, US First Army; Admiral Sir Bertram Ramsay, Allied Naval Commander; Air Chief Marshal Sir Arthur Tedder, Deputy Supreme Commander; General Dwight D Eisenhower, Supreme Commander; General Sir Bernard Montgomery, Commander of Land Forces; Air Chief Marshal Sir Trafford Leigh-Mallory; and Lieutenant General W Bedell Smith.

RIGHT: Eisenhower and Montgomery pose for the camera, their expressions belying the unhappy nature of their relationship.

BELOW: Lieutenant General Omar Bradley, deep in thought aboard the USS *Augusta* as she nears the Normandy coast at dawn on 6 June 1944. The next few hours were to be the most testing of Bradley's life.

systems. This would take several weeks. Harris and Spaatz, however, had other ideas. They were willing to use their bombers in direct support of the army for a few days after the landings, but had no intention of allowing them to be diverted for several weeks from the assault on Germany.

The 'bomber barons' came up with ingeniously oblique alternatives – such as the bombing of synthetic oil plants and motor factories – which were, in fact, a continuation of existing bombing policy. On 25 March Eisenhower brought them into line. In a hostile and confrontational meeting at SHAEF, Eisenhower threatened to resign unless they agreed to devote their forces to bombing the French railroad system. Eisenhower's resignation would have jeopardized not only Anglo-American relations but the entire conduct of the war. Spaatz and Harris were forced to capitulate and in early April the bombing of France began in earnest. Over the next nine weeks Allied air forces flew more than 200,000 sorties and dropped nearly 200,000 tons of bombs. Lancasters and B-17s pulverized rail centers and marshaling yards, then turned their attention to the fortresses of the Atlantic Wall. By the start of June, medium bombers had destroyed 74 of the 92 German radar stations constructed behind the Wall to monitor air movement on and over the English Channel. The Germans were now almost sightless.

The Last Exercises
Invasion had to come soon. By spring 1944 some British and Canadian divisions had spent the better part of three years in training. Efficiency had peaked, and 'overtraining' had started to set in: the jadedness which comes when exercises become well-rehearsed rituals bearing no apparent relationship to reality. Some of the troops had already seen much,

SECRET

[handwritten:] also Erhkey
H.M. *[illegible]*
[illegible]
F.M. *[illegible]*

PROGRAM

PRESENTATION OF 'OVERLORD' PLANS

A. M. 15 MAY

Subject	Speaker	*[handwritten: Eisenhower]*	Time of Presentation
Introduction	Supreme Commander		10 minutes (beginning at 1000 hrs)
General Army Plan	C-in-C, 21 Army Group	*[handwritten: Montgomery]*	30 minutes
General Navy Plan	ANCXF	*[handwritten: Ramsay]* *[handwritten: Ramsay]*	30 minutes
General Air Plan	Air C-in-C, AEF		40 minutes
Strategical Air Forces Plan	Joint presentation: Commanders USSTAF and Bomber Command		30 minutes
General Administrative Plan	C.A.O., SHAEF		30 minutes
Civil Affairs Plan	AC of S, G-5, SHAEF		20 minutes (Conclude presentation at 1330 hrs)

Total time allotted for presentation   3 hours 10 minutes
Intermissions for changing maps, etc.   40 minutes
TOTAL TIME ALLOTTED   3 hours 50 minutes

P. M. 15th MAY

Subject	Speaker	Time of Presentation
NCWTF Tactical Plan	Admiral Kirk	1 hour (Beginning at 1430 hrs) (Division of time as agreed by the three speakers
First Army Plan	General Bradley	
9th Air Force Tactical Plan	General Quesada	
NCETF Tactical Plan	Admiral Vian	1 hour (Division of time as agreed by the three speakers. Conclude presentation at 1730 hours.
Second Army Tactical Plan	General Dempsey	
21 TAF Tactical Plan	A.V.M. Broadhurst	

Total time allotted for presentation   2 hours
Intermissions for changing maps, etc.   40 minutes
TOTAL TIME ALLOTTED   2 hours 40 minutes

SECRET

TOP SECRET

WITH THE COMPLIMENTS

OF

ALLIED NAVAL COMMANDER,

EXPEDITIONARY FORCE.

Rear Admiral W.R. PATTERSON, C.B., C.V.O.
2nd Cruiser Squadron.

AEF

GOOD FOR DATE ABOVE ONLY!

ABOVE: Operation Fabius, May 1944. US infantrymen storm ashore on Dorset's Slapton Sands. Two nights after this photograph was taken, German E-boats annihilated an American landing convoy and by dawn hundreds of bodies had been washed up on the sands.

LEFT: The agenda for one of the most famous briefings during World War II, the meeting in the model room at St Paul's School on 15 May 1944, where, for the first time, the Allied High Command briefed its political and military masters on the details of the invasion.

RIGHT: In their part of Operation Fabius, British troops wade ashore from LCTs near Southampton.

perhaps too much, action. Famous British formations like the 51st Highland and 7th Armoured Divisions had fought from Egypt to Italy, via Libya, Tunisia and Sicily. They had suffered very heavy casualties and were not looking forward to storming the Atlantic Wall. Most American divisions, with the exception of a few such as the 29th Infantry, stationed in England since 1942, were far more recent arrivals in the theater. They were enthusiastic soldiers, but anxious and generally inexperienced.

Salisbury Plain and Exmoor may have been fine for training armored formations, but by early 1944 some realistic amphibious exercises were needed. Five seaside locations were chosen for Operation Fabius – areas which resembled the French beaches, namely Slapton Sands in Dorset, the Gower peninsula in Wales, and Burghead Bay, Culbin Sands and the Tarbat peninsula in Scotland. Operation Fabius shocked officers and men out of their complacency. The exercises were marred by malfunctioning equipment, traffic jams, collisions at sea and general confusion. When a flotilla of German E-boats from Cherbourg attacked an American convoy of LSTs exercising off the Slapton Sands, Allied forces were given a painful reminder of the enemy's military capabilities. The Germans damaged several landing craft and sank two of the LSTs, inflicting over 1000 dead on the Americans. After the Slapton Sands massacre, morale at SHAEF sank. Would Overlord be another Gallipoli or Dieppe?

The Final Plans

On 15 May 1944, the model room of London's famous St Paul's School housed a portentous meeting. For the first time ever, Eisenhower unfolded Overlord in all its complexity before a select audience including the Prime Minister, the King, the CIGS and scores of admirals, generals and air marshals. On D-Day, now set for 5 June, no less than eight divisions were to land in Normandy, three from the air and five from the sea. Two American airborne divisions, the 82nd and 101st, were to drop at night along the eastern coast of the Cotentin peninsula to secure the western flank of the beachhead. Meanwhile the British 6th Airborne Division was to land east of the River Orne.

The other five divisions were to land on five different beaches – codenamed respectively Utah, Omaha, Gold, Juno and Sword – running from west to east between the areas secured by the airborne forces. The US 4th Infantry Division was to land on Utah, the westernmost beach at the base of the Cotentin peninsula; the US 1st Infantry Division on Omaha, the area roughly between the heavily-defended Pointe du Hoe and Port en Bessin; the British 50th Infantry on Gold, the area from Arromanches to La Rivière; the Canadian 3rd infantry on Juno, which lay between La Rivière and Luc; and the British 3rd Infantry Division on Sword.

When the sun set on D-Day, the Allies planned to control a stretch of the Normandy coast 80 kilometers long and some

ABOVE: The workhorse of the invasion forces was the LCT, capable of carrying five tanks and up to a company of infantry. Unfortunately there were never enough of them, and most infantry landed from the more vulnerable LCVPs.

RIGHT: US signalers practising their communications; the Aldiss lamp was used for ship-to-shore contact and the 'walkie-talkie' radio for communication with troops inland.

LEFT: A US Sherman engineer tank is put through its paces on Slapton Sands. Unlike the British, the Americans had few such tanks, something which, on 6 June, many were to regret.

16 kilometers deep. The British would have secured Caen and Bayeux, important communication centers. Meanwhile the Americans would be on the point of pivoting to the north-west to take the port of Cherbourg from the landward side. Once ashore there was to be a rapid and massive build-up, to be made possible by the arrival of the Mulberry harbors from D+3 onward. The 17 divisions in Normandy would expand rapidly to 39 divisions by D+90. By that time, the bulk of Allied forces would have broken out and would be well across the Seine, heading for the Low Countries and the Sieg-fried Line.

Operation Fortitude

The die was cast, but what if the Germans got wind of the plans? Overlord could turn into one of the greatest massacres in history. Ever since COSSAC had been established, activi-ties connected with the invasion had been shrouded in the greatest secrecy. But secrecy alone was not enough. The Allies needed an active rather than a passive security strat-agem: one that would mislead and deceive the Germans into concentrating their forces in the wrong area before D-Day. All nations have tried their hands at deception operations: the British seem to have a peculiar enthusiasm and a genius for the task, but when each separate service and some semi-independent agencies threw themselves into the business of deception, chaos ensued. Churchill, who took a close personal interest in these developments, saw the need for a central deception agency. Thus LCS was born, the London Controlling Section, which could restrain some of the wilder schemes and co-ordinate various operations into a smoothly running whole. The whole process became so large that it had its own codename – 'Fortitude'.

Fortitude was designed to mislead the Germans into believing that the Allies would land at the Pas de Calais. The Normandy landing, even after it had taken place, had to look like a mere diversionary tactic for the 'real' invasion. The LCS used the full force of its ingenuity in creating an entirely ficti-tious army in Kent for German consumption. All genuine radio traffic generated by the 21st Army Group in south-central and southwest England was sent over land lines to the southeast and rebroadcast. Meanwhile, the fields of Essex and Suffolk blossomed with huge encampments crammed with rubber blow-up tanks and airfields packed with mock-up transports made from wooden three-ply. Former German agents who had been 'turned' and were now man-aged by MI5, broadcast plausibly accurate reports of the vast extent of these encampments. The reports seemed confirmed by the behavior patterns of British agents under observation in Sweden, Switzerland, Spain and Portugal. MI6 operatives were seen trawling the local bookshops for all the Michelin maps of the Pas de Calais they could find. Fast-flying German reconnaissance aircraft, FW-190s, stripped of armor and guns, swept over eastern England in broad daylight at 800 kph, cameras clicking. The blurred photographs seemed to confirm that this was indeed the real invasion army. So great was Fighter Command's mastery of the air space over England that German reconnaissance aircraft which tried to penetrate over south-central and southwest England in day-light usually failed to return. By the late spring all sources of intelligence, particularly the sharp eyes of the Resistance, in-dicated that Fortitude was working.

'OK, Let's Go'

During May last-minute preparations got underway. At the start of the month Admiral Ramsay warned Eisenhower of an impending delay: not all the vital LSTs had yet arrived from America; however, Eisenhower's naval staff advised him that best-possible tidal conditions would occur during the week beginning Monday 5 June. This was the date set for D-Day. May 1944 proved to be a beautiful month over southern England – the skies were blue and cloudless, the temperature well above average, and the English Channel was like a mill-pond. All over England the roads to the south-coast ports were choked with military convoys, some over 160 kilo-meters long. The coastal zone of the south and southwest was now closed to civilians: once the troops entered this area they were out of contact. The gigantic machine was at last in motion, an avalanche of men and materiel.

Only one thing could stop it now: the weather. As England continued to bask under a near-tropical sun, the com-manders became anxious. On 30 May Churchill asked the First Sea Lord: 'How does this hot spell fit in with our dates? Does it tend to bring about a violent reaction or is it all clear ahead? Let me have the best your meteorologists can do . . .' Eisenhower grew obsessed by weather reports, but by the evening of 31 May he was beginning to relax.

A few hours later the weather broke – rain and wind gust-ing to gale force swept over the English Channel, accom-

ABOVE RIGHT: 'It's the real thing this time.' US troops crammed into an LCI on 3 June 1944, some forcing a cheery smile for the camera, others looking grim and apprehensive. Within 24 hours most of these men would be desperately seasick, longing for their ordeal to end one way or the other.

RIGHT: Empty LCVPs waiting to pick up their complement of US infantry from a Devon port on 3 June. Clouds are banking up to the southwest, showing ominous signs of the dreadful weather to come.

LEFT: Watched by the antiaircraft gunners of the USS *Ancon*, a convoy of LCIs steams into the English Channel on the evening of 5 June 1944. The lowering clouds and bronzed sea indicate the unsettled nature of the weather.

LEFT: A US half-track is loaded into an invasion barge on 3 June. US forces put ashore many such vehicles in the first hours of the invasion, most of which would not be used in the fighting for several weeks.

BELOW LEFT: US troops march along the promenade of a Devon seaside resort on 2 June. That weekend most towns along the south coast of England witnessed similar scenes.

BELOW: US troops board assault vessels somewhere in southern England, 5 June. Note the barrage balloons.

panied by heavy, scudding cloud. Over the next 72 hours the weather continued to deteriorate. On Saturday 3 June Eisenhower reiterated preparation orders for a 5 June landing, but in the face of deepening worries. He slept little for the next 48 hours. At 0415 hours on Sunday 4 June the forecast for Monday 5 June was for mounting seas, poor visibility, and low cloud over the Normandy beaches. The Supreme Commander had no choice – he brought the huge machine grinding to a halt.

The situation was now desperate. American convoys destined for Utah Beach were already at sea off Cornwall observing radio silence; coastal command had to send out aircraft to ensure their return. Conditions on the crowded transports became appalling. Even in the Solent's sheltered waters they rolled and lurched, causing violent seasickness among the troops. Those crammed below decks could barely cope with the overwhelming stench of vomit.

Few commanders have ever faced such a terrible dilemma. Eisenhower knew that if he canceled Overlord it would take at least a month before conditions would be right again: a month in which morale would drop and the edge go from the men's training, a month in which the Germans might manage to penetrate Operation Fortitude and redeploy their forces. If he made the decision to go ahead, the result might be the greatest disaster of maritime history, a twentieth-century version of the destruction of the Spanish Armada. At 0400 hours on 5 June meteorologists predicted a 24-hour abatement in the bad weather, beginning in the early hours of Tuesday 6 June. Admiral Ramsay and General Montgomery, also present, were convinced that the operation should go ahead. With the nonchalance of a Kansas farm boy leaving for a barn dance, Eisenhower gave the most momentous order of World War II: 'OK, let's go.'

4

D-DAY

As dusk fell on 5 June, convoys of packed trucks and jeeps carried 20,000 men of the US 82nd and 101st Airborne Divisions and the British 6th Airborne Division to airfields throughout southern England and the Midlands. The paratroopers, heavily laden with equipment, weapons and parachutes (37 kilograms or more was a typical load) struggled into 1400 waiting transports. Other airborne troops without parachutes were detailed to embark on the 3500 gliders waiting to be towed to France. Weather conditions that night over southern England and northern France were miserable: drizzle and squalling winds gusting up to near gale force.

By 2230 hours British double-Summer Time, the night sky over England's south coast reverberated to the roar of airplane engines as wave after wave of squadrons headed south. Shortly after midnight, transports carrying the 82nd and 101st swung east across the English Channel toward the Cotentin peninsula. They suddenly hit a storm of antiaircraft fire. The Dakota pilots took evasive action, ducking and diving, and within minutes the formations had broken up. Pilots,

uncertain of their bearings, nevertheless gave the paratroopers the order to jump. Some of the 101st dropped down directly into streams of flak. A *Time* magazine correspondent with the 101st relayed the horrible fate of one man:

'A 20mm shell hit him in the belly. Fire caps in his pockets began to go off. Part of the wounded man's load was TNT. Before the human bomb could explode, his mates behind him pushed him out. The last thing they saw of him, his parachute had opened and he was drifting to earth in a shroud of bursting flame.'

Many of the 82nd and 101st died in the descent. Hundreds of others were deposited far from their drop zones. Weighed down by equipment and tangled in their parachutes, they plummeted into flooded fields and soon drowned. Those who made it down relatively unscathed blundered around in the dark trying to form their units. Major General Maxwell Taylor, commander of the 101st, landed all alone in a field and scouted around before he found his men.

The 82nd were equally scattered, but by a curious quirk of

ABOVE: American airborne forces suffered heavy casualties in the parachute drops on the night of 5-6 June. Most were not as fortunate as these wounded paratroopers of the 82nd Division.

RIGHT: First contact with the locals. An American paratrooper offering chewing gum to French children in the village of St Marcouf, close to Utah Beach.

LEFT: Paratroopers of the 82nd Airborne Division storming the church at Ste Mère Eglise on the morning of 6 June.

LEFT: Skirmishing in and around St Mère Eglise went on for several days. Lieutenant Colonel Edward Krause's men not only had to keep the Germans out but also had to deal with still-active snipers in parts of the village.

RIGHT: Their faces etched with strain, paratroopers of the British 6th Airborne Division await the signal to jump.

RIGHT: The full kit of an American paratrooper weighed more than 90 kilograms, close to the maximum weight any well-trained healthy young man could carry. Those paratroopers who had the misfortune to land in inundated areas drowned.

the wind, about 30 paratroopers landed right on top of their primary objective, the town of Ste Mère Eglise. This was less lucky than it seemed. An earlier bombing raid had set part of the town ablaze and as the paratroopers descended, silhouetted black against the orange night sky, German troops picked them off, killing or capturing most. One man parachuted down onto the church steeple and hung there, pretending to be dead; after two-and-a-half hours of being deafened by the church bells he was taken prisoner. Another 100 men landed on the outskirts of the town. They were rapidly organized by Lieutenant Colonel Edward Krause, then fought their way into and captured Ste Mère Eglise, spending the rest of the day fighting off German counterattacks.

The drop may have been chaotic but, for all that, the scores of small bands of heavily-armed paratroopers posed serious problems for the German defenders, the 709th and 91st Divisions. They were so widely scattered that the Germans found

it impossible to focus on a target. A group of paratroopers surprised and killed the 91st's commander as he returned from an exercise.

While the Americans were landing on the Cotentin, the spearhead of British 6th Airborne approached its landing zone. Six gliders carried an assault party of the Oxford and Bucks Light Infantry commanded by Major John Howard which was tasked with seizing the bridges over the Caen Canal and the Orne River, the eastern boundary of the British beachhead. At 0030 hours on 6 June the first glider crash-landed 47 meters from its objective, the impact hurling the pilot, Staff Sergeant J Walborough, forward out of the cockpit. He was the first British soldier to land on French soil; unfortunately he was unconscious. Exactly one minute later, the second glider plowed down behind Howard, the pilot calling to his passengers, 'We're here, piss off and do what you're paid to do.'

Within seconds Howard and his paratroopers charged at the bridge with bloodcurdling screams. Forty years later a German survivor could still feel the terror that had gripped him on seeing them hurtling toward him:

'I'm not a coward, but at that moment I got frightened. If you see a para platoon in full cry, they frighten the daylights out of you. And at night-time when you see a para running with a Bren gun, and the next with a Sten, and no cover round my back, just me and four youngsters who had never been in action, so I could not rely on them – in these circumstances you get scared.'

The first part of 6th Airborne Division's operation was an unqualified success. Within minutes they had taken the bridge, but holding it would prove harder. It would take several hours for the Allied landing forces to come ashore and reach the Orne. The first German counterattack came before dawn:

a tank attack without infantry support. Sergeant Wagger Thornton sat in a ditch on the east side of the river with a Projector Infantry Anti Tank (PIAT), an extraordinary springloaded antitank weapon. He recalled:

'You're a dead loss if you try to go farther. Even 50 yards is stretching it, especially at night. Another thing is that you must never, never miss. If you do you've had it because by the time you reload the thing and cock it, which is a bloody chore on its own, everything's gone, you're done. It's drilled into your brain that you mustn't miss. And sure enough, in about three minutes, this bloody great thing appears. I was more hearing it than seeing it, in the dark.

It was rattling away there, and it turned out to be a Mark IV tank coming along pretty slowly, and they hung around a few seconds to figure out where they were and what was happening ahead. Only had two of the bombs with me.

LEFT: Staff Sergeant Walborough's glider, with the bridge over the Caen Canal (shortly to be known as Pegasus Bridge) only 50 meters away in the background. This brilliant piece of navigation allowed Major John Howard's assault party to capture its objective within minutes of landing.

LEFT: US paratroopers move through the main street of a Normandy village (St Marie-du-Mont) after linking up with the US 4th Infantry Division on Utah Beach.

Told myself you mustn't miss. Anyhow, although I was shaking, I took an aim and bang, off it went. I hit him round about right bang in the middle. I was so excited and so shaking I had to move back a bit.'

The rest of 6th Airborne had been coming down farther east – 68 gliders of the 5th Parachute Brigade landed at Ranville, about two kilometers from the bridge over the Orne. Eighteen gliders were completely destroyed when they ran into the extensive pole-and-wire network 'bird-traps' put up by the Germans. The famous Australian war correspondent Chester Wilmot who flew in with the 5th Brigade recorded the scene:

'With grinding brakes and creaking timbers we jolted, lurched and crashed our way to the landing in northern France early this morning. The glider in which I traveled came off better than most. The bottom of the nose was battered in . . . the wing and the tail assembly were slashed

TOP: These men of Lieutenant Colonel Terence Otway's 9th Parachute Battalion were more fortunate than many. Scattered over a wide area, scores of others drowned in the swamps along the Dives River. These four fell into the hands of the Germans, and were happy just to be alive.

ABOVE: British commandos and paratroopers link up on D-Day.

RIGHT: Immediately on landing to the east of the Orne, the troops of the British 6th Airborne Division dug in to secure the eastern flank of Sword Beach. They spent much of 6 June isolated and under heavy German attack.

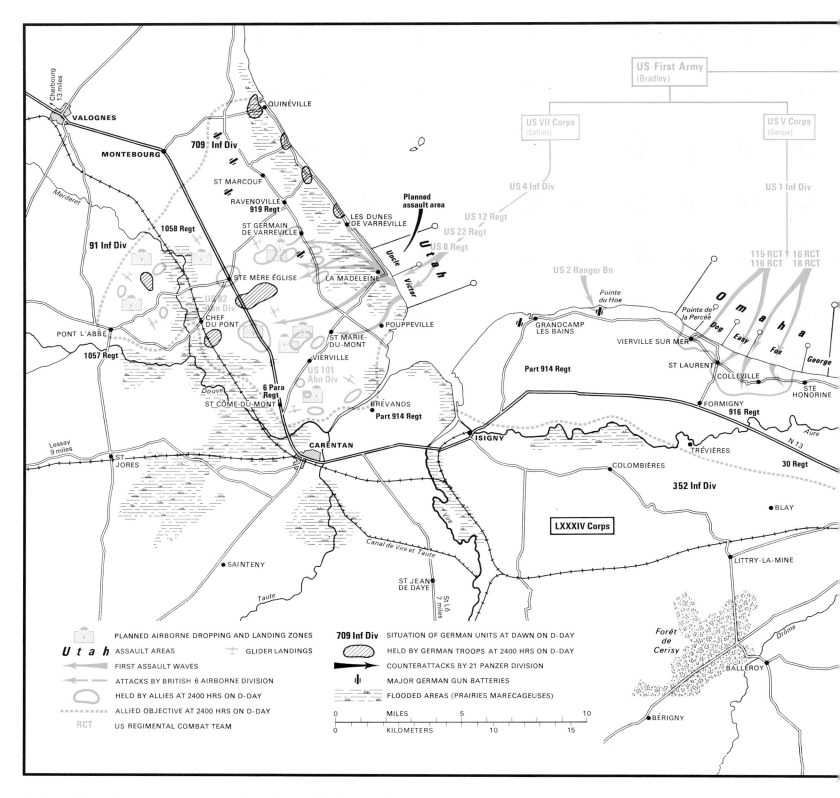

PLANNED AIRBORNE DROPPING AND LANDING ZONES

U t a h ASSAULT AREAS

FIRST ASSAULT WAVES

ATTACKS BY BRITISH 6 AIRBORNE DIVISION

HELD BY ALLIES AT 2400 HRS ON D-DAY

ALLIED OBJECTIVE AT 2400 HRS ON D-DAY

RCT US REGIMENTAL COMBAT TEAM

GLIDER LANDINGS

709 Inf Div SITUATION OF GERMAN UNITS AT DAWN ON D-DAY

HELD BY GERMAN TROOPS AT 2400 HRS ON D-DAY

COUNTERATTACKS BY 21 PANZER DIVISION

MAJOR GERMAN GUN BATTERIES

FLOODED AREAS (PRAIRIES MARÉCAGEUSES)

here and there, but she came to rest on her three wheels, even though she had mown down five stout posts that came in her path, and virtually crash-landed in a plowed field.

No one was even scratched. We shouted with joy and relief and bundled out into the field. All around we could see silhouettes of other gliders, twisted and wrecked – making grotesque patterns against the sky. Some had buried their noses in the soil; others had lost a wheel or a wing; one had crashed into a house, two had crashed into each other.'

The divisional commander, Major General Richard Gale, came down near Wilmot. As he climbed out of his wrecked glider, his eyes met the chaotic scene. They soon moved on to the next field where a chestnut horse grazed. Gale, a fine horseman, caught it, and rallied his scattered forces.

Eight kilometers east, heavy enemy flak met the Dakotas carrying Lieutenant Colonel Terence Otway's 9th Parachute Battalion heading for an assault on the German's coastal battery at Merville. The planes were forced to weave and dive. The flight formations disintegrated; when the battalion came down they found themselves scattered over a wide area. Scores of paratroopers drowned when they dropped

down straight into the swamps of the Dives River. By 0300 hours Otway was able to muster only 155 men, but without heavy equipment. He should have been able to count on 600, with mortars, antitank guns, and jeeps.

The vital priority was the destruction of the 150mm guns covering the beaches. Otway, unable to wait any longer, led the rump of his unit in a furious frontal assault. By dawn, the battery was in British hands. The paratroopers destroyed three guns with demolition charges. Once these were exhausted, they used two shells, fired simultaneously, to destroy the fourth; 110 dead and wounded Germans lay piled up in the bunkers and entrenchments, but British casualties were also heavy. Otway lost 65 men, dead or wounded.

Operation Neptune

By 0300 hours the invasion fleet was just off the Normandy coast. Two midget submarines were only a few hundred meters off-shore. From their conning towers just above sea level, naval officers flashed lights to guide the flotillas of minesweepers clearing passages toward the beaches. To the north lay a huge armada of ships, more than had ever been assembled at any one time in the whole of history. Over 2500 square kilometers of the English Channel were crammed with

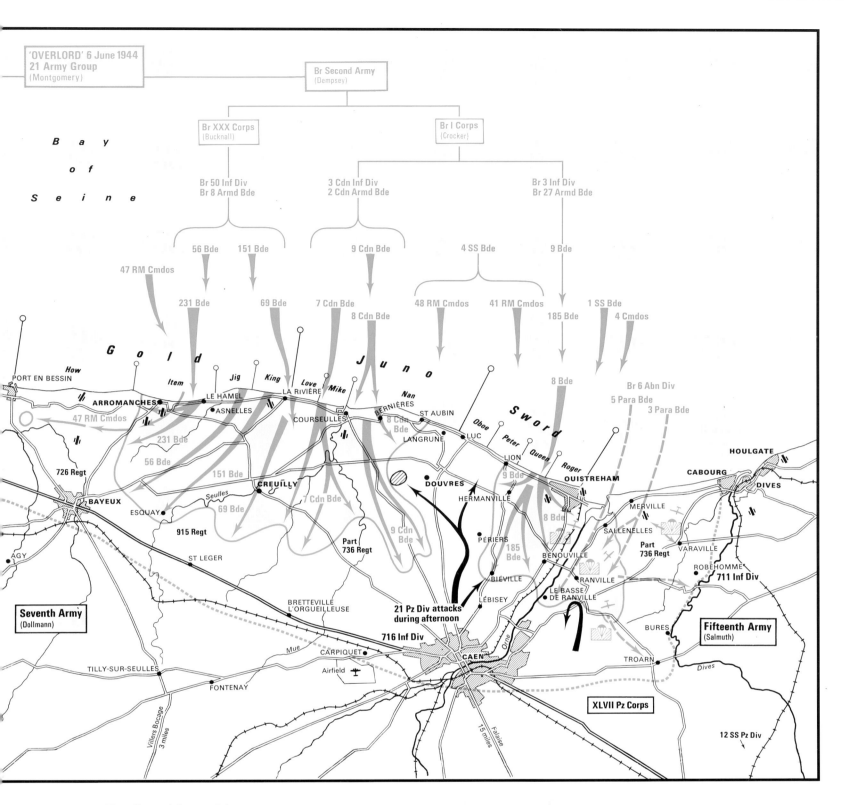

'OVERLORD' 6 June 1944
21 Army Group
(Montgomery)

Br Second Army
(Dempsey)

Br XXX Corps
(Bucknall)

Br I Corps
(Crocker)

Br 50 Inf Div
Br 8 Armd Bde

3 Cdn Inf Div
2 Cdn Armd Bde

Br 3 Inf Div
Br 27 Armd Bde

56 Bde

151 Bde

9 Cdn Bde

4 SS Bde

9 Bde

47 RM Cmdos

231 Bde

69 Bde

7 Cdn Bde

8 Cdn Bde

48 RM Cmdos

41 RM Cmdos

185 Bde

1 SS Bde

4 Cmdos

B a y

o f

S e i n e

G o l d

J u n o

S w o r d

How
PORT EN BESSIN

Item

Jig

King

Love
Mike

Nan

Oboe

Peter
Queen

Roger

8 Bde

Br 6 Abn Div
5 Para Bde
3 Para Bde

HOULGATE

ARROMANCHES

LE HAMEL
ASNELLES

LA RIVIÈRE

COURSEULLES

BERNIÈRES

ST AUBIN

LUC

LION

OUISTREHAM

CABOURG

DIVES

47 RM Cmdos

231 Bde

8 Cdn
Bde

LANGRUNE

9 Bde

8 Bde

MERVILLE

726 Regt

56 Bde

151 Bde

CREULLY

Seulles

DOUVRES

HERMANVILLE

9 Bde

SALLENELLES

BAYEUX

ESQUAY

69 Bde

7 Cdn Bde

PÉRIERS

BÉNOUVILLE

Part
736 Regt

VARAVILLE

915 Regt

Part
736 Regt

9 Cdn
Bde

185
Bde

ROBEHOMME

711 Inf Div

AGY

ST LEGER

BIÉVILLE

RANVILLE

BURES

LÉBISEY

LE BASSE
DE RANVILLE

BRETTEVILLE
L'ORGUEILLEUSE

21 Pz Div attacks
during afternoon

Fifteenth Army
(Salmuth)

Seventh Army
(Dollmann)

716 Inf Div

TROARN

Dives

Mue

CARPIQUET

ORNE

CAEN

TILLY-SUR-SEULLES

Airfield

Falaise

*Villers Bocage
3 miles*

FONTENAY

15 miles

XLVII Pz Corps

12 SS Pz Div

ABOVE: The dispositions of the
rival forces and the Allied
objectives on D-Day.

RIGHT: Laden with British
vehicles and troops, an LCT
approaches the French coast.
The large number of soft-
skinned logistics vehicles which
the Allies landed on 6 June
reflected the high command's
belief that they would soon be
engaged in maneuver warfare
deep in the interior of France.

7000 ships carrying 287,000 men. These included 1213 warships, ranging in size from battleships to torpedo boats, 138 of which were tasked with bombarding the coast. The largest of these were three American and four British battleships, and 23 British, American, French and Polish cruisers.

By 0500 hours the bombardment squadrons were in position. Ten minutes later the cruiser HMS *Orion* opened fire on the German battery at Mont Fleury. Over the next 20 minutes 1000 naval guns, ranging in caliber from 16- to 4-inches, fired on every known German battery along the 96-kilometer stretch of coast, from Villerville in the east to Barfleur in the west. Twenty-two kilometers off Villerville, the British battleship *Warspite* directed its 16-inch guns onto three German destroyers nosing their way out of Le Havre. The odds were ludicrous, yet within minutes *Warspite*'s guns had demolished one of the destroyers. The other two fled back into the port. On the task force's western side, the American battleships *Arkansas, Nevada* and *Texas,* alongside the French cruisers *Montcalm* and *George Leygues,* pounded targets along Omaha and Utah Beaches.

Utah Beach

Utah and Omaha were the westernmost beaches. H-hour for landing here was set at 0630 hours, one hour after low tide. Farther east, along the British beaches where the tide came in later, H-hour was set for 0730 hours. As the first light of dawn gleamed over Utah Beach, troops of the US 4th Division clambered down landing nets into their LCTs for the more than 10-kilometer trip to the beach. The 28 DD Sherman tanks, buoyed up by inflatable canvas skirts, looked like huge floating boxes as they bobbed and plunged in the choppy sea.

As the landing craft approached to within six kilometers of the beach, they met a barrage of German shells. Just before 0600 hours, Patrol Craft (PC) 1261, the boat guiding the assault forces to their landing beach, was hit and went down by the stern. About 4400 meters from the coast, the landing craft were caught in a strong lateral current running off the beach. The bombardment had also obscured traces of landmarks vital to navigation. All of these factors meant that when American troops waded ashore at 0631 hours, they were 1700 meters south of their intended landing site.

LEFT: Barrage balloons flying aloft to protect ships from the Luftwaffe, the troops of the US 4th Division are transported toward Utah Beach.

BELOW: Minesweepers of the Royal Navy clear the way for the American landing by exploding mines off Utah Beach.

RIGHT: A fortunate error in navigation brought US forces ashore on Utah Beach more than a kilometer south of their intended objective. Waterproofed jeeps drive through the shallows bringing supplies for the infantry.

BELOW: Troops of the US 4th Division's 8th Regiment wade ashore on Utah Beach shortly after 0630 hours, 6 June. German resistance in this sector was very light.

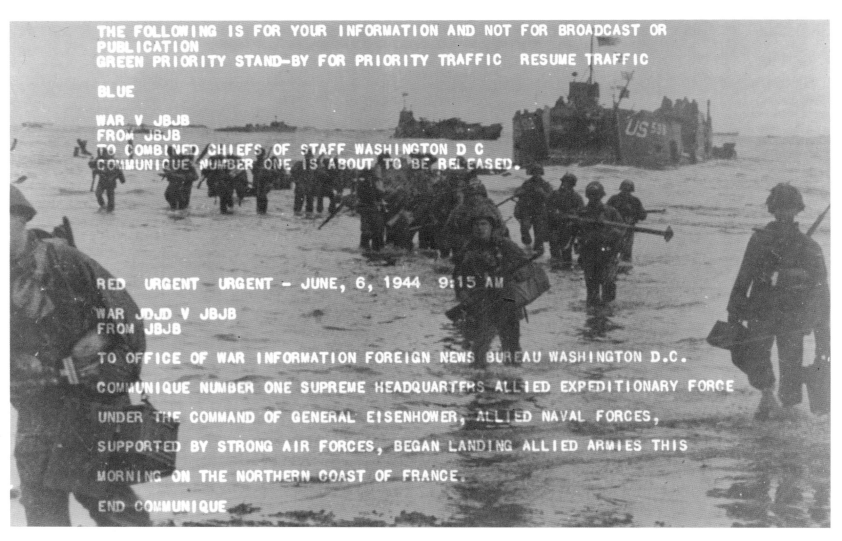

THE FOLLOWING IS FOR YOUR INFORMATION AND NOT FOR BROADCAST OR PUBLICATION
GREEN PRIORITY STAND-BY FOR PRIORITY TRAFFIC RESUME TRAFFIC

BLUE

WAR V JBJB
FROM JBJB
TO COMBINED CHIEFS OF STAFF WASHINGTON D C
COMMUNIQUE NUMBER ONE IS ABOUT TO BE RELEASED.

RED URGENT URGENT - JUNE, 6, 1944 9:15 AM

WAR JDJD V JBJB
FROM JBJB

TO OFFICE OF WAR INFORMATION FOREIGN NEWS BUREAU WASHINGTON D.C.

COMMUNIQUE NUMBER ONE SUPREME HEADQUARTERS ALLIED EXPEDITIONARY FORCE

UNDER THE COMMAND OF GENERAL EISENHOWER, ALLIED NAVAL FORCES,

SUPPORTED BY STRONG AIR FORCES, BEGAN LANDING ALLIED ARMIES THIS

MORNING ON THE NORTHERN COAST OF FRANCE.

END COMMUNIQUE

ABOVE: The text of Eisenhower's message from SHAEF, announcing to the world that the liberation of Europe had begun.

LEFT: Troops of the US 1st Infantry Division embarking in southern England. Their destination is Omaha Beach.

BELOW: Smiling troops of the US 2nd Ranger Battalion pictured before their perilous assault on Pointe du Hoe.

This accident proved rather fortuitous as the section of beach they had landed on was virtually undefended, and they met only light resistance. They later discovered that the beach they had intended to land on was covered by two still-functioning batteries. The Americans advanced inland along a causeway built through the coastal marshes. By 0930 hours they were within three kilometers of Ste Mère Eglise; to the rear, wave after wave of the 4th Division were landing.

Pointe du Hoe

A very different situation faced American troops to the east, just across the Vire estuary. The concrete emplacements atop the Pointe du Hoe jutted out like the towers of a medieval castle. They were thought to house six heavy guns – guns which could wreck the Utah or Omaha landings. The Allies had repeatedly bombed the headland: since 0500 hours, the USS *Texas* had been busy pounding it, but there was only one way to make certain the guns had been knocked out.

Three companies from the 2nd Ranger Battalion, commanded by Colonel James Rudder, were to land at the foot of the cliff, scale it, then knock out the German position. The destroyers USS *Satterlee* and HMS *Tarlybant* closed to within 3500 meters of the cliffs and opened up at virtually point-blank range on the German emplacements. At this point the Rangers reached the cliff base. The German defenders, troops of the 352nd Division, anticipating commando assaults, had booby-trapped the cliff edge with 240mm shells hooked at 100-meter intervals with tripwires. The Rangers may have been highly trained and at the peak of their physical fitness, but it was an almost impossibly daunting task. Naval gunfire, however, kept the Germans in their

ABOVE RIGHT: Their rifles slung or at the trail, GIs of the US 22nd Regiment, 4th Division, wade ashore near La Madeleine on Utah Beach. So far all was well but a few kilometers inland there was to be much heavy fighting.

RIGHT: US Rangers rest at the foot of the cliffs at Pointe du Hoe, while medics treat the wounded.

LEFT: A lieutenant of the US 116th Regiment attempts to catch a glimpse of Omaha Beach while his men huddle in the LCVP. They are still far enough away from the shore not to have experienced the effect of German fire.

RIGHT: About 700 meters offshore, most LCVPs grounded on a hitherto undetected sand bar.

BELOW RIGHT: Heavily-laden GIs head for Omaha Beach. Few in the first assault waves made it.

bunkers and cut the wires, so that it was impossible to explode the shells. From the beach below, the Rangers fired up rockets attached to grappling hooks and rope ladders which arced up over the cliffs. As the naval gunfire lifted, the Rangers swarmed up the ladders. The Germans came out of the bunkers and showered them with grenades. Some exploded, toppling Rangers from their ladders, but the Rangers fielded many, lobbing them back over the cliff top.

The Rangers were strong, agile and lightly equipped; soon they had reached the cliff top and were over, fighting their way across a moonscape of craters and twisted wreckage caused by bombs and naval gunfire. It was all over very quickly. The Rangers took Pointe du Hoe at a cost of only 40 casualties; the 155mm guns had unfortunately been moved inland, though the Rangers later found and destroyed them.

Omaha Beach

American troops landing at Omaha to the east faced a different set of problems. The transports had anchored 19 kilometers offshore, half as far again as they had anchored off Utah. The wind scudding in from the northwest made this stretch of water far rougher than Utah – much too rough for the clumsy landing craft. The heavily-laden troops of the 116th Infantry Regiment of the US 1st Division and the 16th Infantry Regiment of the US 29th Division clambered down scaling nets into the rolling and plunging landing craft. As they pulled away, loaded to the brim, the waves came crashing down on them. Within minutes 10 were completely swamped. Most of the 300 men on board were drowned. Some craft managed to keep afloat, but only just, men bailing out furiously with their helmets. The larger LCTs with their cargos of DD tanks, seeing the difficulties the landing craft were in, closed to within 5400 meters of the shore before releasing their cargo. Even in good conditions, the DD tanks had a freeboard of less than a meter. Some of the waves were over two meters high, and 27 out of the 29 tanks were soon

swamped. They sank down like stones, carrying their crews to the bottom. It was a useless sacrifice and the Americans wisely canceled the launching of any more, although this meant that the infantry would be landing without any support at all. The novelist Ernest Hemingway, working as a war correspondent, was aboard one of the LCTs:

'As the LCVP rose to the crest of a wave, you saw the line of low, silhouetted cruisers and the two big battlewagons lying broadside to the shore. You saw the heat-bright flashes of their guns and the brown smoke that pushed out against the wind and then blew away. Those troops who were not wax-gray with seasickness, fighting it off, trying to hold onto themselves before they had to grab for the steel side of the boat, were watching the *Texas* with looks of surprise and happiness.

There would be a flash like a blast furnace from the 14-inch guns of the *Texas* that would lick far out from the ship. Then the yellow-brown smoke would cloud out and, with the smoke still rolling, the concussion and the report would hit us, jarring the men's helmets. It struck your ear like a punch with a heavy, dry glove.

Then up on the green rise of a hill that now showed clearly as we moved in would spout two tall black fountains of earth and smoke. "Look what they're doing to those Germans," I leaned forward to hear a GI say above the roar of the motor. "I guess there won't be a man alive there," he said happily. That is the only thing I remember hearing a GI say that morning.'

The GI could not have been more wrong. Smoke and low cloud meant that much of the naval support fire failed to find a target. The men in the first LCVPs realized that the Germans were far from dead when they heard machine-gun bullets spatter against the steel ramps of their craft before it grounded. The tide was out – in some places it was nearly two kilometers to the beach. The troops, weighed down with heavy equipment, landed in neck-deep water and slowly

struggled toward the shore in the face of increasingly heavy fire. Some took cover behind concrete obstacles, some lay half-submerged at the water's edge, unable to get across the bullet-swept sand to the relative safety of the sea wall. *Life* magazine's Frank Capa, who went in with the first wave, lay among the bodies in the shallows, shooting off all the film in his camera. He only shot the one reel: his hands were shaking so violently that he could not reload the camera. As the tide began to come in, many of the wounded lying around Capa drowned.

On Omaha Beach all semblance of command and control had now gone. At the top of the beach stood a low stone sea wall, the edge of a seaside esplanade, beyond which lay sand dunes and concealed German positions. Beneath it huddled small groups of wounded, frightened men, the few who had made it up the beach, now sheltering from the unremitting wave of German fire which swept over the beach and breakers. As waves of troops continued to land the scene turned to chaos.

More and more landing craft and men piled up in the shallows, hundreds of American bodies floated along the beach, bobbing like flotsam in the incoming tide. An order canceling further landings caused worse confusion as the LCTs and LSTs circled around amid shell- and machine-gun fire. Hemingway, now ashore, described the nightmarish scene:

'On the beach on the left . . . the first, second, third, fourth and fifth waves lay where they had fallen, looking like so many heavily-laden bundles on the flat pebbly stretch between the sea and the first cover. I saw three tanks coming along the beach, barely moving, they were advancing so slowly. The Germans let them cross the open space where the valley opened onto the beach, and it was absolutely flat, with a perfect field of fire.

Then I saw a little fountain of water jut up, just over and beyond the lead tank. Then smoke broke out of the leading tank on the side away from us, and I saw two men dive out of the turret and land on their hands and knees on the stones of the beach. They were close enough so that I could see their faces, but no more men came out as the tank started to blaze up and burn fiercely.'

By 0900 hours the situation on Omaha was appalling. On the bridge of the command ship, USS *Augusta*, a desperate Lieutenant General Omar Bradley sent SHAEF an urgent message asking permission to abandon the beachhead. A communications foul-up meant that Eisenhower did not receive it until late in the day, by which time the situation had changed. The Navy played a crucial role in preventing a complete disaster. At 1030 hours two landing craft, LCT 30 and LCI (L) 544, steamed full ahead through the obstacles off the beach opposite Colleville on the eastern side, firing all their weapons at enemy strongpoints. Even after they had been grounded they continued to pour fire on enemy positions at near point-blank range.

At the same time two destroyers came broadside on to within 1000 meters of the beach. With their keels scraping the bottom they pumped broadside after broadside of 5.2-inch shells into German positions at Moulins on the beach's western side. German fire began to slacken. One of the few surviving senior officers, Colonel George A Taylor, commanding the 16th Infantry, rallied the small knots of survivors within earshot: 'Two kinds of people are staying on this beach, the dead and those who are going to die. Now let's get the hell out of here!'

A few men, sickened by the carnage and now more angry than afraid, charged after the colonel into the dunes. More followed. One soldier started up an abandoned bulldozer. He drove up the beach, plowed through a minefield, filled in an antitank ditch, and began carving away a sand dune. Elsewhere the same process was underway. Small parties of Americans fought their way off the beach and pushed inland. Badly organized and unsupported by artillery and tanks, they were lucky to meet Germans in the same state of disarray. Throughout the day skirmishing took place in the hedgerows around Vierville-sur-Mer, St Laurent and Colleville.

LEFT: Survivors of an LCVP which sank off Omaha Beach coming ashore in a rubber life raft. The sea was high, and many of the landing craft were swamped on their way in. Others were holed by the mined underwater obstacles.

TOP RIGHT: A section from 47 Commando of the Royal Marines. These tough, well-trained assault troops landed on the western flank of Gold Beach and immediately set out to link up with the Americans on Omaha.

ABOVE RIGHT: Commandos move through the hamlet of St Comen de Fresne, halfway between Gold and Omaha Beaches.

RIGHT: British infantry and paratroopers inspect a knocked-out German blockhouse at Le Hamel on Gold Beach late on 6 June.

Gold Beach

The slaughter on Omaha had been going on for more than an hour when 16 landing craft set out for the western flank of Gold Beach, to the east of Omaha. They carried the first British troops, 47 Royal Marine Commando. Here German fire was even more intense: shells screamed down, hitting most of the craft. The tide was now well in; the craft maneuvered crazily between the half-submerged obstacles and then grounded well up the beach, only 100 meters or so from a sea wall.

As the bullets spattered the steel ramps, a clear British officer's voice was heard above the din, insouciantly asking another, 'I say, do you think we were intruding? This seems to be a private beach.' It diffused the real terror of the moment. The ramps crashed down. In a flash, the lightly-equipped commandos were across the beach to the relative safety of the sea wall. They suffered just 43 casualties. Showers of grenades and mortar bombs saw off the German defenders, and soon the commandos were well inland, circling around behind the heavily-defended Arromanches. At 0800 hours, they reached the hamlet of St Comen-de-Fresne, halfway between Gold and Omaha.

Farther east, units of the British 50th Division, the Hampshires and the Dorsets, were vomiting their way through a terrible bout of seasickness, but unlike the Americans off Utah, their mood was buoyant. Each landing craft had a Tannoy from which blared popular songs of the day, such as 'Roll Out the Barrel' and 'We Don't Know Where We're Going.' Above the din of the engines and the gunfire, thousands of voices could be heard singing 'the gang's all here . . . we'll have a barrel of fun.' Sadly we have no record of what the Germans thought of all this, but it probably confirmed their long-standing doubts about British sanity.

Gold Beach, a continuation of Omaha, resembled it very closely, but this landing was going to be very different. Unlike the Americans, the British decided that it was too rough to launch the DD tanks at sea. Instead the LCTs came into the

shore. Losses were heavy. German shells plunged amongst the LCTs and hit 20, but many more made it to the beach. The ramps lowered. Instead of the expected infantry, the waiting German machine-gunners were stunned to see monstrous armored vehicles emerging, the 'Funnies' of the 79th Armoured Division. Crab tanks flailed paths through the minefields up the beach, oblivious to the metallic scream of the machine-gun bullets spraying around them.

At Le Hamel, in the center of Gold, a German 88mm anti-tank gun in a concrete bunker (missed by both the aerial and naval bombardment) blasted away at incoming landing craft. A Crab commanded by Sergeant Lindsay, RE, which landed to the east of Le Hamel smashed through the center of the still strongly-defended town, firing and flailing alternately, until it came up alongside the emplacement. Edging his tank around to the front, Lindsay (in 79th Division parlance) 'posted a letter': he swung the muzzle of his gun into the embrasure, fired, and blew the '88' and its crew out of the back.

When the soldiers of the Dorsets and Hampshires landed, they found 79th Division tanks hard at work. Infantry casualties were mercifully light. By 1030 hours British troops had pushed inland to a ridge, while others, supported by the Funnies of the 79th Division, proceeded to reduce German strong points in Le Hamel and La Rivière. By this time, the 8th Armoured Brigade, a component of 7th Armoured Division, was also coming ashore, and the British were starting their drive southwest toward Bayeux and due west toward the Americans on Omaha Beach.

Juno Beach

The Canadian 3rd Division, landing farther east on Juno Beach, had a tougher time. From the outset, German shelling was intense: 90 of the 306 landing craft were sunk or damaged. Only 14 DD tanks of the Canadian 1st Hussars, launched at 3600 meters in very rough seas, finally made it to the shore. They came in well ahead of the Funnies or the infantry, and went into action against the beach defenses.

One of the assaulting units, the Regina Rifles, was supposed to land with the tanks to the east of Courseulles, but its A Company landed too far to the west, right in the town center. The DD tanks were positioned off to the left, and rough seas delayed the arrival of the Funnies. So troops here had to get through the minefields at the risk of being blown sky-high. A terrible dilemma faced the Canadians: should they advance and risk death on the mines, or stay put and be machine-gunned at the water's edge? One gallant dash ended with 15 mangled bodies lying in the sand. Many died, but the Canadians got into Courseulles, and began methodically clearing the Germans from the houses.

In contrast, the North Shore (New Brunswick) Regiment's landing at St Aubin had gone like clockwork. The amphibious tanks of the Fort Garry Horse were launched from only 1700 meters out, and although the skirts were inflated and propellers engaged, commanders reported that 'it was really a wet wade' to the shore. They arrived simultaneously with the infantry and together they advanced inland.

Unfortunately, the same precision did not mark The Queen's Own Rifles' landing just to the east at Bernières-sur-

Mer. When its B Company landed opposite one of the town's strong points, the DDs and Funnies had yet to be launched. As soon as the ramps were lowered, German machine-gun fire sliced through the packed landing craft. Heavy casualties also afflicted the supporting unit, the Régiment de la Chaudière (known throughout Canada as the 'Chauds'). At 0930 hours four of the Chauds' five landing craft were hit and the majority of the regiment had to swim and wade ashore.

By this time the Queens were street-fighting their way through Bernières-sur-Mer, and the Chauds quickly joined in. Local citizens were astounded to be greeted in what sounded like French in the old Norman dialect. By 1400 hours, the entire Canadian 3rd Division was ashore and pushing south. It advanced rapidly, taking hundreds of prisoners; as dusk fell, some units were more than eight kilometers from the coast.

LEFT: By the time these troops of the Canadian 3rd Division landed on Juno Beach the worst of the fighting was over. Earlier waves had taken very heavy casualties.

RIGHT: British troops on Gold Beach shelter behind their vehicles from German shelling.

BELOW: The first German prisoners being marched back to La Rivière on Gold Beach. The Allies had made arrangements to look after tens of thousands of prisoners but at first they captured only hundreds. The close combat which characterized fighting in Normandy made it difficult for both sides to accept surrenders.

Sword Beach

Sword Beach, the destination of the British 3rd Division, lay the farthest to the east. Allied planners, worried about the gap between Juno and Sword which would be left by the main Canadian and British landings, decided to land 48 and 41 Royal Marine Commandos on either side. There were two reasons for this: first, to protect the right flank of 3rd Division; second, to form a pincer to isolate any German units, and to facilitate the merging of the Juno and Sword beachheads.

Problems hit 48 Commando as soon as it approached the coast opposite St Aubin at around 0900 hours. Five of the landing craft struck mines, and one was hit by shellfire. By the time they reached the beach, 48 Commando was only 200 men strong. This handful of survivors pushed inland. They managed to take the village of Langrune, but further attempts to push eastward were halted by strong German resistance. 41 Commando, landing about six kilometers farther east, had an easier time getting ashore, but soon bogged down in the face of heavy German fire.

On the extreme eastern edge of Sword Beach, opposite the town of Ouistreham, Lord Lovat's 1st Commando Brigade landed at the same time as the first DD and flail tanks. A Royal Naval Reserve officer, Denis Glover, commanding one of the landing craft, later remembered the thoughts that streamed through his mind as they approached the shore:

'We are on those bristling stakes. They stretch before us in rows. The mines on them look as big as planets. And those gray nose shells pointing toward us on some of them look like beer bottles. Oh God, I would be blown up on a mine like a beer bottle.

Whang – here it comes – those whizzing ones will be mortars – and the stuff is falling around us. Can't avoid them, but the mines and collisions I can avoid.

Speed, more speed. Put them off by speed, weave in and out of those bloody spikes, avoid the mines, avoid our friends, avoid wrecked craft and vehicles in the rising water and get those troops ashore.

Slow ahead together. Slow down to steady the ship, point her as you want her, then half ahead together and on to the beach with gathering rush. Put her ashore and be damned! She's touched down. One more good shove ahead to wedge her firm. Smooth work! Now off you go!'

The first troops onto the beach were Commandant Jean Kieffer's Free French Commando Battalion. A mortar bomb fell in the midst of one platoon as it charged from its landing craft, killing or maiming most of them. Kieffer led his men

TOP: 48 Commando coming ashore at St Aubin.

ABOVE: Lord Lovat's 1st Commando Brigade lands on Sword Beach at Ouistreham.

LEFT: Free French commandos fight through the heavily-defended streets of Ouistreham toward the casino.

TOP RIGHT: Lord Lovat's commandos push inland toward Pegasus Bridge.

ABOVE RIGHT: The commandos bypassed most German strong points. When they could not be avoided, Lovat's men made short work of them.

RIGHT: Smiling commandos give the 'thumbs-up' sign.

into the streets of Ouistreham, systematically clearing the town, villa by villa. The Free French attack ground to a halt in front of Ouistreham's casino, converted into a fortress by the Germans. Kieffer managed to make his way back to the beach. When he returned, he led the Funnies of 79 Squadron, AVREs mounting the Petard, the mortar firing the formidable explosive 'garbage can.' After just a few rounds of fire from the Petard the German defenses cracked. The commandos stormed into the casino, and captured the dazed and frightened survivors.

While Kieffer's men fought in the streets of Ouistreham, the bulk of the commandos under Lord Lovat pushed inland. They were aiming to link up with the by-now hard-pressed paratroopers. The route they followed had been carefully selected by Resistance intelligence reports and, as the men moved rapidly to the southeast, they avoided main roads and major strong points, keeping to hedgerows and farm tracks. From midday, they began to hear the noise of battle, first distant, then more loudly, coming from the Ranville area: the staccato chatter of the paratrooper's Bren guns intermingled with the tearing scream of the German MG-42s. Lord Lovat – perhaps remembering the last time a Campbell had come to the relief of a beleaguered garrison, that of Lucknow during the Indian Mutiny in 1857 – ordered his piper to play 'Blue Bonnets over the Border.' Shortly before 1300 hours the commandos and paratroopers joined up. Thanks to the piper, the paratroopers had known for the last half-hour that help was on the way. It arrived just in time. The paratroopers, ammunition almost gone, now rallied to fight off yet another furious German onslaught.

The Commando assaults on Sword were outstandingly successful, but the bulk of the British 3rd Division had a very much harder time. As the bombardment of the warships began to lift, the shore approaches were a turmoil of weaving craft and wreckage. The BBC correspondent Howard Marshall was in one of the landing craft:

'As we drove in we could see shell bursts in the water along the beach and, just behind the beach, we could see craft in a certain amount of difficulty because the wind was driving the sea in with long rollers and the enemy had prepared antiinvasion, antibarge obstacles sticking out from the water – formidable prongs, many of them tipped with mines, so that as your landing barge swung and swayed in the rollers, and they're not particularly manageable craft, it would come in contact with one of these mines and be sunk. That was the prospect that faced us on this very lowering and difficult morning as we drove into the beach.

And suddenly, as we tried to get between two of these tripart defense systems of the Germans, our craft swung, we touched a mine, there was a loud explosion, a thundering shudder of the whole craft, and water began pouring in.'

On Sword Beach, chaos reigned. Crab tanks flailed their way up from the landing craft. German '88's, dug in west of Ouistreham, hit tank after tank, until the whole beach seemed a mass of burning armor. More vehicles kept on landing. By mid-morning, the Crabs had cleared four lanes through the minefields, but by this time a massive traffic jam had built up. The South Lancashires, the advance regiment for 8th Brigade, took some time to extricate themselves from the confusion.

It was mid-afternoon before they were able to push two kilometers inland to Hermanville and Périers Ridge. Here they ran into German antitank guns and dug in. The tanks of the Staffordshire Yeomanry, tasked with reaching Caen, cleared the beach very late in the day and linked up with the Shropshire Battalion. By 1600 hours they had reached Biéville, barely six kilometers short of Caen. Many weeks were to pass before they advanced any farther. Already the German tanks were counterattacking.

5

'THEY'VE COME AT LAST'

The bad weather which set in on 3 June came as a welcome respite to the Germans. On the 5th, the rain descended in sheets, while fierce winds whipped up the breakers, driving them onto the coast. The likelihood of an invasion attempt seemed so remote that Rommel confidently drove off that morning from his headquarters at La Roche-Guyon. He had arranged a personal interview with Hitler at Obersalzburg and intended to break the trip with an overnight stay with his family at Herrlingen, near Ulm, in southern Germany.

His Chief of Staff, General Hans Speidel, was looking forward to a few days of relative peace and quiet. He had planned a dinner party that night for a number of visiting academics and journalists. The commander of the Seventh Army, General Friedrich Dollmann, seemed equally confident that there would be no invasion. On 5 June his headquarters at Le Mans emptied, as staff officers left for a war game at Rennes in Brittany; the city was also the destination for many of his divisional commanders and their staffs. One of Dollmann's commanders, General Erich Marcks of LXXXIV Corps, did, however, stay behind at his head-

quarters in St Lô to attend a birthday party his staff had arranged in his honor. Here, they gossiped into the night, drinking large quantities of an excellent Chablis.

Just before midnight, there were ominous signs that something extraordinary might be about to happen. Radio stations in the Pas de Calais region picked up coded messages; they realized that one signaled an imminent invasion. Radar picked up intense activity in the English Channel. The commander of the Fifteenth Army, General Salmuth, immediately put his forces on full alert, convinced that any attempted landing would take place in his area, the Pas de

BELOW: It was from a position such as this, looking over Utah Beach, that German defenders first sighted the Allied armada. Their reports of thousands of ships heading straight for them were initially disbelieved.

RIGHT: The British press carried a remarkably accurate account of the invasion on the evening of 6 June, omitting only the location of the landings.

Evening Despatch Tue. 6 June 1944

BLACK.WHITE
Ii's the Scotch

Black-out: 11.10 p.m. to 5.2 a.m.

CODE LETTER FOR TO-NIGHT **A**

Moon: 10.0 p.m. to 5.57 a.m.

Evening Despatch

6·30 CITY

No. 16,504.   *Straits: Sun after rain*   TUESDAY, 6 JUNE, 1944.   Radio: Page 3.   ONE PENNY.

INVASION GOING WELL: TANKS ASHORE

ALLIES HAVE FOOTHOLD: SLASHING INLAND

Churchill reveals *ALL TO PLAN—AND WHAT A PLAN*

11,000 planes and 4,000 ships engaged

Our invasion is "proceeding to plan—and what a plan." This is what a confident Mr. Churchill told the House of Commons to-day in a brief review of the landings in Northern France which began soon after dawn.

AN IMMENSE ARMADA OF "UPWARDS" OF 4,000 SHIPS, WITH SEVERAL THOUSAND SMALLER CRAFT, HAVE CROSSED THE CHANNEL, SUSTAINED BY ABOUT 11,000 FIRST-LINE AIRCRAFT, DISCLOSED THE PREMIER.

Massed airborne landings have been successfully effected behind the German lines, landings on the beaches are proceeding and the fire of shore batteries has been largely quelled.

"Obstacles which the Germans had constructed in the sea have not proved to be as difficult as was apprehended," concluded Mr. Churchill.

HITLER TAKES OVER

HITLER HAS TAKEN PERSONAL COMMAND OF ALL THE GERMAN ANTI-INVASION OPERATIONS. REUTER'S MILITARY CORRESPONDENT, WHO SAYS THIS NEWS REACHED LONDON FROM UNDERGROUND SOURCES, ADDS THAT HE IS SURROUNDED BY A STAFF INCLUDING FOUR MARSHALS—RUNDSTEDT (TITULAR COMMANDER-IN-CHIEF), ROMMEL (INSPECTOR-GENERAL), SPERRLE (IN CHARGE OF AIR FORCES), AND BLASKOWITZ (ACTING DEPUTY TO ROMMEL).

Hitler, concludes the correspondent, is believed to have moved his H.Q. to a place somewhere in Northern France.

BERLIN REPORTS ALLIED LANDINGS ON THE CHANNEL ISLANDS OF GUERNSEY AND JERSEY, AND ADDS THAT THE INVASION FORCES HAVE LANDED TANKS ON THE FRENCH MAINLAND 15 MILES NORTH-WEST OF CAEN.

A Reuter message from a U.S. photo reconnaissance base this afternoon says that the Allies have established beach-heads in Northern France and are "slashing inland."

U.S. TROOPS IN VAN

Washington announces that specially-trained and picked assault teams of the U.S. Army made the initial attack, knocking out pillboxes and other fortifications.

At 9.33 a.m. No. 1 communique from Supreme H.Q., Allied Expeditionary Force (SHAEF), told the world that the great day had arrived in these words:—

"UNDER THE COMMAND OF GEN. EISENHOWER, ALLIED NAVAL FORCES, SUPPORTED BY STRONG AIR FORCES, BEGAN LANDING ALLIED ARMIES THIS MORNING ON THE NORTHERN COAST OF FRANCE"

In this brief manner the United Nations, their enemies, and the peoples of neutral nations, heard that "D-Day" had arrived, and that the first stage in the liberation of Europe had begun.

Landings on Guernsey, Jersey

The landings in Normandy, which were preceded by the heaviest attack ever by Bomber Command on German batteries along the French coast, was reported first by Berlin.

The biggest minesweeping operation in history, which paved the way for our landing craft, involved 70 miles of sweep wire and 10,000 officers and men.

S.H.A.E.F. states that more than 640 naval guns, from 16in. to 4in., are bombarding the beaches and enemy strong points in support of the armies.

Allied landings, it is understood in London, were made in Normandy between 6 a.m. and 8.15 a.m. Minesweepers cleared the way.

Naval bombardments, in which U.S. ships took part, were carried out, and airborne landings made, first reports being described as "good."

For three hours before General Eisenhower released the momentous news, German radio stations had been reporting "the invasion," with long accounts of battleships and destroyers off the mouth of the Seine, airborne landings in Normandy, and air attacks on the vital coast between Cherbourg and

Then came the German High Command communique, which said:

"The long prepared and expected attack on Western Europe by the enemy began last night.

"It was initiated by heavy air attacks on our coastal fortifications.

"The enemy dropped air-borne troops at several points on the coast of Northern France, between Havre and Cherbourg, and at the same time carried out sea-borne landings, supported by strong naval forces.

"Fierce fighting is going on in the coastal stretches which have been attacked."

Later a German report said that tanks had been landed in the region of Arrumanches (small fishing village 15 miles north-west of Caen). More than 200 craft approached this part of the coast nine hours after the first landings.

"The enemy is trying to scale the steep coast with the aid of special ladders," it was added.

Robert Reuben, Reuter's special correspondent, was due to go into Europe in one of the leading planes in the airborne units.

He tells of last-minute scenes among the parachutists in a despatch sent from the field of departure Somewhere in England.

Vast numbers of paratroopers, airborne pilots, glider pilots, glider troops and other personnel have been sealed in this airborne area of England (he writes). They are completing last minute preparations. Everyone is now " briefed."

"You have given your commanding officer grey hairs trying to keep you out of the guardhouse," the C.O. told his troops, "but this is one night when I want you to raise all the hell you can.

" I want you to go through your area tearing up and blowing down everything you get your hands on.

"You will be dropped on the back of the Boche—I know you're going to strike terror in his heart."

Before the assaulting troops embarked, each man was handed a copy of a stirring Order of the Day, in which Gen. Eisenhower told his men that the eyes of the world were on them, and that "the hopes and prayers of liberty-loving people everywhere march with you."

"WE WILL ACCEPT NOTHING LESS THAN FULL VICTORY," ADDED THE SUPREME COMMANDER.

"GOOD LUCK AND LET US ALL BESEECH THE BLESSING OF ALMIGHTY GOD UPON THIS GREAT AND NOBLE UNDERTAKING."

A German radio commentator described Portsmouth, Plymouth, Bristol, Hull and the London docks as the "springboards of invasion."

General Montgomery, who is in command of the land forces of British, Canadians and Americans, was in confident mood when he talked to correspondents on the eve of the landings, according to Doon Campbell, Reuter's correspondent at the General's Headquarters.

"The party," he said, "is in first-class shape to win the match. I don't know when the war is going to end, but I don't believe the Germans can go on much longer with this business."

THE KING TO BROADCAST

THE King is to make an invasion broadcast at 9 o'clock to-night.

Gen. de Gaulle, who has been in this country some days, is to broadcast a message to the people of France.

General de Gaulle is accompanied by Mr. Duff Cooper, General Bethouard, Chief of Staff, and the following members of his staff: Col. Billotte, M. Palewski, M. Soustelle, M. Alphand and M. de Courcel.

BIRMINGHAM PRAYED

GREY-HAIRED women with shopping bags, young office girls, workmen with oily hands, and business men were among the many who knelt in prayer in St. Martin's Church, Birmingham, at lunch time to-day.

A discreet handkerchief appeared here and there as the curate, Mr. Garrett, prayed for "absent loved ones."

The shoulders and blonde head of a girl in the back pew shook a little. And a sudden shaft of sunlight burnished the Royal Engineers badge on her handbag.

Across the road from the church a big crowd swarmed round a newspaper seller who was struggling to reach his "pitch."

Very few of his prospective customers secured papers. One of the lucky ones stood on the corner reading invasion news aloud from his copy to his less fortunate colleagues, who jostled round, craning over his shoulder.

EIGHT DAYS' RATIONS

Food provisions for eight days plus one day's emergency rations were put aboard the landing vessels. Each man was issued with a day's emergency rations for the first day's operations until field kitchens will be in operation.

Luftwaffe kept away

THE greatest air fleet ever to assemble for one operation, and probably outnumbering the Luftwaffe by at least three to one, is covering the invasion, says an air correspondent. During the night and since the landings were made Allied bombers and fighter-bombers have been pouring thousands of tons of bombs on the enemy positions.

More than 1,300 R.A.F. up their reinforcements. Over heavy bombers helped to pave the beach-head hordes of the way for the landings by all Allied fighters, flown by all a tremendous six hours' members of the United pounding of German batteries Nations, have formed an between 11.30 last night and umbrella to protect the landsunrise. This was the ing ships and troops from the heaviest-ever attack on these Luftwaffe. batteries.

Ten attacks were made, They have roped off the each by 100 or more bombers. whole battle area, and the Throughout the night, too, only ticket of admittance is formations of R.A.F. Second the white star of the Tactical Air Force concen- liberating armies. trated on road and rail com- Gault McGowan, representmunications. Other Bomber ing the Combined British Command planes without loss Press, reporting from an struck at the railway centre English airfield after watching at Osnabruck in North-west the Second Front start from Germany. the air, said to-day:—

Fighters are to-day casing The situation seems to be tremendous havoc with their that "the Luftwaffe cannons as the Germans bring has not yet put in an appearance in strength.

We landed at low tide to miss mines & under-water obstacles

THE first point upon which some explanation may appear to be necessary is the fact that the landings occurred at low tide, writes our military correspondent.

High-water on the other side of the Channel was shortly after midnight. The troops went ashore between six o'clock and 8.15.

Under-water obstacles were the reason for the fact that the "touch down" occurred in daylight rather than at dawn.

For a long time the enemy has been fixing obstacles below the high-water mark and attaching mines to them.

The chance of landing craft being able to clear them were remote and the decision therefore lay between risking their effectiveness at high tide or giving the landing forces the long approach up the exposed low glacis of the beaches.

Successful

The bare announcement that the landings have been made is an indication that the part of the joint Navies has been successful.

Ahead of the great convoys went the minesweepers, clearing not only channel for the assault troops, but the areas in which the ships making the preliminary bombardment were to operate. Scanty reports to hand suggest that

this part of the operation went well, with little interference from enemy surface craft.

It is now the task of the sweepers to guard against further mining by enemy aircraft. The seas in the neighbourhood of the landings are unlikely to be open to the enemy vessels ever again.

The sappers will also be busy demolishing the underwater obstacles so that full use of the beaches can be made at high water.

Enemy air reaction to the assault so far is unknown and though the air-borne troops are understood to have been dropped with few casualties the nature of their mission cannot yet be stated with precision.

The character of the ultimate objectives of the present stage of the invasion may be judged from the locality in which the landing was made. The hope now is that the Allied Air Forces will be able to prevent the movement of reserves at least until to-night.

Show is "on"

At the time of landing it was believed that the enemy garrisons on the coastal strip were not numerous, but of course circumstances are greatly in their favour.

They will be holding strong points and concrete emplacements which may not have been destroyed in

the preliminary bombardment, and the task of knocking out coastal guns has not been easy.

But the show is "on," and there can now be no drawing back. Weather is all-important over the next few days.

According to early reports it was not particularly favourable during the night, the sea was choppy, and, of course, the variability of tides is a disadvantageous factor.

Men with experience of combined operations in the Mediterranean, which is tide-less, say that the assault across the Channel must have been infinitely harder both to plan and to execute.

DAWN FOR GREATEST EVER ARMADA

This is part of the greatest armada the world has ever known pictured by a British official photographer flying in a plane as the gigantic fleet of warships, transports, landing craft and supply ships waited the signal which has launched the assault for the liberation of Europe. The large transport in the forefront is crowded with assault troops, who within only a few hours were storming the enemy beaches. Assault craft which took part in the great Dunkirk in reverse stretch as far as camera can see.

Off to bed

Never still for a moment. What energy they use! Now it's time for that long refreshing sleep— a cup of OXO and off to bed.

OXO
prepared from PRIME RICH BEEF

Calais. Von Rundstedt in Paris approved this measure but, given the severity of weather conditions, decided that there was little point in alerting forces elsewhere.

Senior German officers were sound asleep when reports of sporadic clashes with paratroopers started to trickle into divisional quarters throughout Normandy, but erratic radio communications, and the destruction of a large part of the French telephone network, made such reports impossible to confirm. Confirmation came in more direct form to the commanding officer of the German 711th Division, Major General Josef Reichart. As he played cards with his staff in his headquarters, he saw two British paratroopers land on his lawn. Other generals were less fortunate. American paratroopers ambushed and killed the unsuspecting Major General Falley of the 91st (Luftwaffe) Division based in Carentan as he drove south to the war game.

At about 0215 hours Speidel was awakened with reports of paratroop landings. He had no information about their strength or scale. When he finally got through to von Rundstedt by phone, who had no clearer information, both men convinced each other that the landings were merely drops to the French Resistance. By 0430 hours a different picture was beginning to emerge. Radio messages and despatch riders were bringing reports that large numbers of ships had been sighted between the Cotentin peninsula and the mouth of the Seine. Von Rundstedt still thought that this was a diversionary tactic and that the real landing would come in the Pas de Calais area, but as a precautionary measure he ordered the 12th SS 'Hitlerjugend' and the Panzer 'Lehr' Divisions to prepare to move up to the Normandy coast.

By 0530 hours, when the first shells from the Allied naval bombardment hit the coast, the hidden meaning of all the coastal activity became blindingly clear, but there was considerable delay in transmitting this news to higher headquarters stationed many miles inland. When Speidel finally managed to get a telephone connection with Rommel at 0630 hours, he was still quite oblivious to the bombardment. He only passed on the reports of the paratroop drops, thereby lulling the Field Marshal into a false sense of security. He soon acquired more definite information, but it took until 1000 hours before he was able to get through to Rommel again to tell him that Allied landings were underway on the Normandy coast. The news galvanized Rommel into action, but it took him most of the day to drive back to his headquarters; Hitler had previously issued an edict forbidding senior German officers to travel by air any longer lest they be shot down.

TOP: The first intimation that the commander of the Wehrmacht's 711th Division had of the invasion was when British paratroopers landed in the middle of his headquarters. They were captured and interrogated.

ABOVE: German prisoners captured on D-Day.

LEFT: In the confused fighting on 6 June many American and British troops fell into German hands. Here a column of Allied prisoners is marched to the rear.

ABOVE RIGHT: German troops atop a self-propelled assault gun move through the Normandy countryside.

Down in Le Mans, General Dollmann's headquarters staff remained ignorant of the landings until 0845 hours, when they received news that British troops were coming ashore opposite Caen; they did not hear about the American landings to the west until 1100 hours. Dollmann believed that these latter landings were diversions, and that the earlier British landings were the main invasion. Von Rundstedt did not share this opinion. Even after he had received definite confirmation of the landings, he continued to believe that they were all feints. The real invasion, he still thought, would soon descend on the Pas de Calais.

This was also Hitler's own view. When the news of the landings reached him at 1000 hours, while he was holding court in Berchtesgaden, he seemed almost relieved. 'They've come at last!' he announced. For the previous two years German forces had been tied down along the Atlantic coast while the Allied Armies remained poised in southern England. Now that the Allies had committed themselves to decisive action, the German Army could crush them. Albert Speer, the armaments minister, was with Hitler on 6 June; his memoirs record Hitler's train of reasoning on that day: 'Do you recall? Among the many reports we've received there was one that exactly predicted the landing site and the day and hour. That only confirms my opinion that this is not the real invasion yet.'

Hitler was at first reluctant to authorize the release of the armored reserve. Meanwhile, German units were fighting desperately all along the coast, but these were battles fought by battalions and companies who had little or no contact with higher headquarters. In some places they did very well. Battalions of the 352nd Division holding the hinterland to Omaha managed to get word back to their divisional commander, Major General Dietrich Kreiss, that they had wiped out the landing on the beaches. Kreiss continued to believe this throughout the day; but by mid-afternoon his troops were running low on ammunition and the enemy was pushing inland.

On the extreme east of the beachhead Major General Edgar Feuchtinger, commanding the 21st Panzer Division (a formation which had served with Rommel in North Africa), sent his tanks against the paratroopers on the Orne bridges before dawn, even though he had not received orders to do so. By 1000 hours the 21st was heavily engaged with the paratroopers and was beginning to gain the upper hand when Feuchtinger received his first message from high command, ordering him to break off the engagement and move to defend Caen. It took the 21st the rest of the morning and the early part of the afternoon to carry out the order. They wasted most of the day disengaging and moving. By mid-afternoon many of Feuchtinger's tanks were very low on fuel, but his logistics officers were unable to contact depots in Caen to have more sent forward. Even so, Feuchtinger's tanks brought the British advance from Sword to a halt at Biéville.

By dusk on 6 June the German response was becoming more co-ordinated. The hardened Panzer reserves, the 12th SS, 2nd SS, Panzer 'Lehr' and 17th Panzer Grenadiers, had been ordered to move toward the beachheads. But it was all too late. For the Germans it had been a bad day. They had misinterpreted the true nature of the landings, a misinterpretation which was in part the result of Operation Fortitude, and in part the result of a catastrophic communications failure between the various levels of command. The troops had generally fought well, but when reinforcements had failed to arrive and when they ran low on ammunition, they had either surrendered or had been overwhelmed. Many Allied leaders had expected a repeat of Gallipoli. Instead 130,000 troops had landed from the sea and another 22,500 had arrived from the air, all for 10,000 casualties, a third of which had taken place on Omaha. For the Allies it had been a good day.

6

FRANCE IN FLAMES

From the morning of 6 June Dollmann's Seventh Army was locked in combat with the British, Canadians and Americans on a 60-kilometer front stretching along the Normandy coast. However, the Germans also had to face another, more insidious army – the French Resistance. By this stage the Resistance was a highly-organized force. Three months earlier de Gaulle had forged the disparate, quarrelsome groups into a single organization, known as the French Forces of the Interior (FFI). The London-based General Pierre Koenig had overall command, while Jacques Chaban-Delmas was appointed to field command in France.

The Resistance could now boast a reliable command, communications and logistics system. After prolonged consultation with the numerous group leaders of the Resistance, Koenig and Delmas had divided France into 12 *delegues militaires regionaux* (DMRs). Each region had a separate command and communications system, which usually depended on three-man Anglo-French Special Operations Executive (SOE) teams. For the first time ever, the Resistance was capable of co-ordinated nationwide action; even more significantly, in certain regions the FFI enjoyed better and more secure communications than the Germans.

By March 1944 the FFI had some 100,000 personnel, the numerical equivalent of about eight divisions. Initially, their strong military potential was hampered by inadequate arms supplies, which were dependent on sporadic parachute drops but, later, regular arms supplies were greatly facilitated by the establishment of an effective command and communications system. Between March and May Allied transport aircraft flew 1665 missions to the FFI, delivering some 7000 tons of supplies and munitions. These included 76,290 Sten guns, 27,961 pistols, 16,945 rifles, 3441 Bren guns, 572 bazookas, 304 PIATs and 160 mortars. In terms of equipment, the FFI paralleled the British and American airborne divisions: light weaponry which, if used properly, could prove highly effective.

However, larger problems concerning the role and effective use of the FFI itself, let alone its weaponry, taxed both the French and other Allied leaders. The Americans and the British viewed the FFI as a purely military organization. Some officers argued that it would be most effectively deployed in staging a series of uprisings of steadily increasing intensity, starting in early summer, which would draw the Germans away from the Normandy coast. De Gaulle and his

LEFT: By May 1944 the French Forces of the Interior (FFI) had become quite formidable and paraded openly in remote areas of central and southern France.

ABOVE: The exiled de Gaulle receives the congratulations of Eisenhower on the occasion of the National Day of France, 14 July 1942.

RIGHT: In the weeks immediately before D-Day RAF Dakotas dropped supplies and Anglo-French SOE teams in many areas of northern France. These gave the FFI the training and weaponry it had so far lacked.

LEFT: Teenagers were the most enthusiastic recruits to the FFI. Having spent their childhood under German occupation, many 16- and 17-year-olds were itching to hit back at the 'Boche.'

RIGHT: Designed by SNCF workmen, this steel clamp attached to a rail was a simple but very effective means of derailing German trains.

BELOW RIGHT: The sleeping quarters in a *Maquis* camp deep in the Massif Central. In the early summer of 1944 crude camps like this sprang up in many remote locations and were to become the sites of several pitched battles.

lieutenants rejected the plan at once: the FFI would incur massive casualties, out of all proportion to any effect it might have on the battlefield. The FFI, supported by many Allied officers, put forward an alternative plan. In the hours preceding the planned Allied landings, the FFI would launch simultaneous strikes throughout northern France, designed to destroy and disrupt the German command, communications and transport systems. SHAEF approved. This inspired scheme carried the rather uninspired title 'Plan A.' 'Plan B' was a similar FFI scheme for the south of France, which was to be initiated prior to the 'Anvil' landings (August 1944).

Plans A and B met with de Gaulle's approval, but the French general harbored far more ambitious long-term plans for the FFI as a potent political force. His attempts to secure Anglo-American recognition of the FFI as the sole legitimate government of France had met with failure. De Gaulle feared that once the landings were over the British and Americans would impose an occupation government upon France, one that might well liaise with collaborationist Vichy officials and might eventually incorporate much of the Vichy apparatus. Some of de Gaulle's plans for the FFI therefore contained an in-built political agenda designed not only to countermand the German forces but also to secure certain regions for future de Gaullist control.

'Plan C' entailed projected FFI uprisings in the more remote and mountainous regions of France. Here the FFI, if aided by supply drops from the British and American forces, would stand a strong chance of challenging German control and thereby detain German forces far from the landing beaches. The remoteness of these regions would, of course, also make them equally suitable for de Gaulle to establish areas of control beyond the reach of the Allies. The Americans and British would thus be presented with a political *fait accompli*. The Free French authorities in Algiers accepted that Plan C would go into effect simultaneously with Plan A. SHAEF in England gave it a lukewarm reception, and promised nothing more than moral support for future uprisings. Thus the scene was set for the finest and most tragic battles of the Resistance.

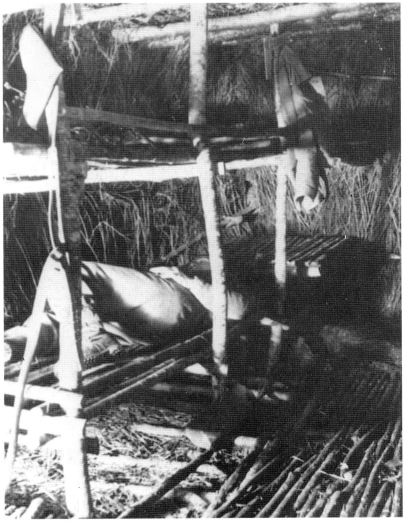

Jour J – Les Batailles du Rail

On the evening of 5 June the BBC's French-language service broadcast 'personal messages' after the news. The broadcasting of personal messages was not unusual: during the preceding four years it had been a useful means of transmitting orders and information to agents. This night was different. It took the announcer more than an hour to read through 325 personal messages. As he intoned, 'I will bring the eglantine', Resistance leaders all over northern France pricked up their ears. They had just heard the code calling for the immediate implementation of the first part of Plan A, Operation *Vert*, the scheme for rail sabotage. As the broadcast continued, other announcements activated the rest of Plan A: Operation *Tortue*, the destruction of bridges and highways, Operation *Bleu*, the disruption of the electricity-supply system, and Operation *Violet*, the cutting of telephone and telegraph links.

Before midnight FFI teams had sprung into action all over France. In the vital area of the Normandy beachheads, the FFI intelligence chief Guilloum Mercader cycled at breakneck speed along coastal roads, carrying orders from team to team. Mercader was a nationally-famous cyclist (he had represented Normandy several times in the Tour de France), and as a goodwill gesture, the Germans had granted him a permit allowing him to cycle through restricted areas. In Caen stationmaster Albert Auge and his men set about disabling the locomotives in the city's marshaling yards.

Farther west teams commanded by a café proprietor, André Farine, cut the telephone cables leading out of Cherbourg. Meanwhile other teams led by Yves Gresslin, a Cherbourg grocer, were dynamiting the railroad lines linking Cherbourg, St Lô and Paris. In Brittany, small teams of the Deuxième Regiment des Chasseurs Parachutistes (RCP), the Free French equivalent of the British SAS, parachuted down to join more than 3500 *Maquisards*. Before the night was out they had cut a swathe of destruction through eastern Brittany. They wrecked bridges and railroad tracks, demolished electricity pylons, and established roadblocks covered by machine-gun and bazooka teams. They took every step to stop the 150,000 German troops in Brittany from reinforcing the beachhead quickly.

Some 600 kilometers away, large sections of the lines radiating from Dijon, the hub of the railroad network in eastern France, erupted in explosions: in all 37 cuts were made. Across the whole of France the first 24 hours of FFI operations succeeded in cutting the rail network in 950 places, causing the derailment of 180 German trains.

As they engaged Allied landing forces, German units in Normandy found confusion and disruption in the rear. As the telephones went dead, German commanders tried to communicate by radio; the Allies then jammed the airwaves and intercepted their messages. Electricity supplies failed in cities as far apart as Caen and Cherbourg. To keep their essential equipment running, the Germans had to resort to generators, which ate up valuable and limited fuel supplies. Their logistics chains broke down; soon ammunition for all sorts of weapons, but particularly the valuable mortars, was in short

ABOVE: When captured by the *Maquis*, collaborators could expect no mercy. This woman, accused of passing information to the *Milice*, was tried, found guilty and executed within a few minutes.

LEFT: The hated *Milice* raid the home of a *Maquis* suspect in February 1944. Four months later the *Milice* were as much a target of the FFI as the Germans.

supply. In many areas the intensity of German fire slackened as commanders, worried by the nonappearance of supplies, conserved stocks.

Les Batailles du Route

Although von Rundstedt remained convinced that the main Allied landing would come in the Pas de Calais, within hours of the landings he had ordered the reinforcement of Normandy. Several powerful German formations began to move toward the beachheads, but derailments and blown-up bridges soon confined movement to the roads. Here the German troops became vulnerable to sniping and ambush. They had to march and fight their way to the beachheads, suffering casualties en route. By the time they finally reached the battlefield, many were desperately in need of rest and resupply.

Had one particular German division, the infamous 2nd SS Panzer Divison, 'Das Reich', managed to get to Normandy by 6 June, the course of battle might have been dramatically dif-

ferent. 'Das Reich' was one of the most formidable formations in western Europe: 20,000 superbly-trained, battle-hardened troops with 240 tanks and self-propelled guns, including 100 Tigers and Panthers. However, on D-Day it was still stuck at Montauban to the north of Toulouse, about 600 kilometers from the beachhead.

On the evening of 6 June the officer commanding, Brigade-führer Heinz Lammerding, received orders to move to Normandy. Under normal conditions the move would have been completed by 9 June, but by that date advance units had only just reached Limoges, still 350 kilometers south of Normandy. The rest of the division was strung out over 260 kilometers of the winding RN20, all the way back to Montauban. Everything had gone wrong for the Germans. Although the division had already been in a high state of alert (in the previous three months it had suffered 200 casualties in clashes with the *Maquis*), on 7 June the Resistance managed to blow up much of its fuel reserves and some of its transport. Panzer grenadiers hastily requisitioned all the fuel and civilian vehicles they could lay their hands on, but the move had been delayed by several hours. The next 48 hours turned into a nightmare. The Resistance ambushed the advance guard on a bridge before Souillac where RN20 crossed the Dordogne, and hit the long flanks of the stalled column in a dozen other places.

The SS were angered and frustrated by the casualties and delays caused by hidden enemies who quickly melted into the mountainous countryside. They retaliated with the same brutal tactics which they had used to quell partisan activity on the Eastern Front. On 9 June Lammerding led a Panzer grenadier battalion into the town of Tulle, 80 kilometers south of Limoges, and caught the citizens in the middle of celebrating their liberation. The SS troopers publicly hanged 99 men, women and children from the balconies of houses along the main street and forced their families to watch.

The following day the advance guard surrounded and then occupied the village of Oradour-sur-Glane, 15 kilometers northwest of Limoges. The SS separated the men from the women and the children, split them into several groups, and machine-gunned them. They herded the women and children into the church, threw in a satchel of high explosives and hand grenades, and then gunned down the survivors as they sought to escape the flames. In all 642 died — 190 men, 245 women and 207 children.

The advance guard pushed north. When it reached the Loire on 11 June, the Germans discovered that only a single-track bridge had survived Resistance sabotage or air attacks. The division following up behind, constantly harassed by Resistance attacks, jammed itself into a bottleneck: a sitting target for air strikes from the medium bombers called in by Anglo-French SOE teams operating with the Resistance. Meanwhile, on 14 June, advance elements reached the division's assembly area at Domfront, 80 kilometers south of the beachheads. It was now that 'cab ranks' of rocket-firing Typhoons, directed in by the SOE, hit 'Das Reich', destroying

BELOW: A scene often repeated during 'Das Reich''s 17-day journey from Toulouse to Normandy.

RIGHT: Unlike the civilians massacred by 'Das Reich', these soldiers of the FFI had at least been tried before their executions.

large bodies of *Maquisards* conducted raids up to 150 kilometers away in the Loire Valley. An entire German division, 12,000-strong, was despatched to deal with them. The Germans struck on 10 June and for the next 10 days a battle raged that was equal in ferocity to anything that was happening on the distant Normandy beachhead. The Resistance destroyed the initial German attack, inflicting 3100 casualties, but the Germans called in an additional 8000 troops with heavy weapons and air support. In the early hours of 21 June the Resistance, running short of ammunition, broke off the battle and withdrew deeper into the Massif Central.

In the southeast another uprising was underway. The steep, thickly-wooded slopes of the plateau of Vercors to the southwest of Grenoble made the area a natural fortress. During the course of 1943 the Resistance had set up many camps in the forest. By 6 June 1944, some 4000 *Maquisards* had assembled on the plateau and had hacked out an airstrip for the Allied transport aircraft they were convinced would soon arrive. Like the *Maquisards* of Mont Mouchet, the men of Vercors raided and carried out demolitions which brought traffic to a halt over wide areas of southeastern France.

The Germans could not ignore an open insurrection. On 13 June they launched a frontal assault which was beaten off with heavy casualties. The following day the Germans launched a set-piece attack – a creeping artillery barrage behind which the infantry advanced and overran the *Maquisards*' outer defenses. The steep slopes of the Vercors, however, proved too much, and the attack bogged down. For the next five weeks the Germans and the *Maquis* waged attritional warfare; increasingly desperate appeals to the Allies for assistance elicited a supply drop on 14 July, but no paratroopers. On 21 July the Germans launched a full-scale, two-division assault supported by air attacks and the landing of glider-borne SS commandos who landed on the airstrip built to take Allied transports. Within days the Germans had overrun the plateau and had annihilated the Resistance.

The largest uprisings occurred at Mont Mouchet and the Vercors, but in the days following 5 June they were supported by many smaller, short-lived insurrections throughout France. Several of these also ended with the extermination of the Resistance. These battles cost the FFI 24,000 dead and perhaps two or three times as many wounded, roughly the same level of casualties suffered by the Allied armies during the first three weeks of the Normandy invasion.

The Frenchmen who fought and died in these battles tied up the equivalent of eight German divisions during the crucial early days of the Allied build-up. Adding to this the smaller-scale interdiction operations of Plan A to the north, the Resistance either delayed or engaged between 12 and 15 German divisions. The FFI made an enormous contribution to the success of the Normandy landings; a contribution not sufficiently appreciated by recent British and American historians of the campaign who have tended to write the Resistance out of history. The Allied generals who commanded in Normandy came to a very different conclusion.

General Omar Bradley, in his autobiography *A Soldier's Story*, stated that he had counted heavily on the Resistance to impede German reinforcements from reaching the beachheads, and that this was the key element in the Allies' ability to hold onto the beaches long enough to build up strength for a break-out. Eisenhower was equally grateful. In August 1944 he told war correspondent David Schoenbrun, 'The French Resistance was magnificent. The railroad men not only kept us informed of all movements but, over and over again, they impeded the transport of German armies, holding them up as much as 36 hours, enough to help turn the tide of battle in our favor, particularly when we were still inside the beachheads of Normandy.' Later, in his *Crusade in Europe*, Eisenhower estimated that the Resistance had been worth 15 divisions to the Normandy landings. He was not being overgenerous.

16 vehicles in the first attack. The full division finally limped into Normandy on 23 June, far too late to influence the battles for the beachhead. It had left in its wake a countryside literally in flames; but far from quelling the Resistance, 'Das Reich' had acted as a very effective recruiter for de Gaulle's forces.

'Das Reich's' march to the beachhead was the most difficult conducted by any German formation, but many other divisions en route to Normandy experienced similar problems. One division took only four days to move from Poland to the French frontier, but then another 20 days to reach Normandy. The Wehrmacht's powerful 'Grossdeutschland' Division and the Luftwaffe's 'Hermann Goering' Division were also ordered to Normandy, but took weeks to effect the move. The German transportation system, both by rail and road, should have moved like a well-oiled machine, but the FFI's Plan A caused massive disruption. From the evening of 5 June onward, nothing worked as it should have done.

Plan C – Insurrection

Plan A had the Allies' full approval; Plan C did not. Nevertheless, on 5 June signals were transmitted which led to full-scale uprisings in south-central and southeastern France. By late May some 10,000 Resistance fighters had gathered in camps in the Mont Mouchet region of the Massif Central. RAF and USAAF Dakotas supplied them with rifles, bazookas and grenades although, apart from a few SOE teams, the paratroopers they were expecting did not arrive. On 6 June

7

BUILD-UP AND ATTRITION

The First Days Ashore

The disruption of German communications bought the Allies several vital days in which to establish the beachhead. In the months preceding the landing, literally millions of man-hours had been devoted to working out complex landing procedures for men and materiel. These plans did not survive the first few minutes on the Normandy beaches; all was chaos. Logistics troops on the beaches formed ad hoc teams and kept the materiel moving to improvised depots. By the end of the first day 8900 vehicles and 1900 tons of stores had been landed on the British forces' beaches alone. It was desperately dangerous work. German batteries at Le Havre kept pumping shells onto Sword Beach, but the biggest blow came not from the German gunners but from RAF Bomber Command: on 7 June a Lancaster bomb-aimer misjudged his target and dropped a stick of bombs onto the main British ordnance depot just off the beach. The result was spectacular, as 26,000 liters of fuel and 400 tons of ammunition exploded.

BELOW LEFT: By 7 June order was emerging on Gold Beach. The Royal Engineers had laid a wire-mesh pathway along the beach and trucks were moving supplies inland. In the picture are some of the two million jerry cans of gasoline and oil which the British brought to Normandy. Unfortunately by the time the break-out was underway two months later most of the jerry cans had been 'acquired' by the troops and put to other uses. The result was a serious logistics problem.

BOTTOM LEFT: Omaha Beach, 11 June. The Americans made spectacular progress in constructing their Mulberry harbor and by 11 June were unloading the first cargo, well ahead of the British. The Royal Navy's engineers were skeptical, some saying that the Americans had sacrificed durability for speed. Events were to prove the Royal Navy right.

ABOVE RIGHT: In the days following 6 June LCTs ran a shuttle service across the Channel, depositing supplies in Normandy and sometimes returning with prisoners. This propaganda photograph suggests that the British were taking large numbers of prisoners but the true number for the first month in France was fewer than 10,000.

CENTER RIGHT: While the Mulberry harbor was under construction the Americans continued to land supplies over open beaches. This wire-mesh driveway runs across the sand and shingle of Omaha Beach. In the background lies a mute reminder of the dreadful events of 6 June — the remnants of an LCVP blown in half by a German mine.

RIGHT: Shortly after D-Day, Lieutenant General Omar N Bradley and the US naval commanders Rear Admiral John L Hall (center) and Rear Admiral Alan G Kirk (in dark naval uniform) landed on Omaha Beach. As they look seaward their grim expressions speak volumes. Although this photograph was taken by the US Navy for publicity purposes, the US censors quite wisely decided not to use it.

ABOVE: A Phoenix caisson being towed into position off Arromanches where it will be sunk to form a breakwater. Unlike the Americans, the British concentrated on building sea defenses before they towed the floating roadways and cranes into position.

LEFT: The American Mulberry at Omaha Beach, 18 June 1944, the floating pier allowing convoys of trucks to drive ashore.

RIGHT: The floating pier at Omaha after the abatement of the 'Great Storm' on 22 June. So great was the damage that American engineers scrapped it and towed the salvageable sections eastward to Arromanches where they were incorporated into the British Mulberry. Thanks to the breakwaters this had survived with relatively superficial damage.

Logistics planners had known that landing men and supplies on open beaches would be a dangerous and uncertain business, and would not produce the military muscle needed to secure the beachhead, let alone allow a break-out. The success of the Normandy landings depended on getting the Mulberry harbors into position as quickly as possible. The first of the 600 caissons and blockships was deposited off Arromanches in the British sector, and off Omaha in the American sector, on 7 June. Eleven days later the American harbor received its first cargo and, by 18 June, 24,412 tons of supplies and ammunition had rolled ashore from the two Mulberries.

The Great Storm

Shortly before dawn on 19 June disaster struck – the worst summer storm in living memory. Lieutenant Commander Taylor was in mid-Channel, commanding a convoy of tugs towing 22 caissons. Never before in a long career at sea had he experienced a storm of such unexpected violence:

> 'It arrived from nowhere, whispering across the water at first and finally rising to a triumphant shout of malignancy calling from the seas an answering mood. It caught the unseaworthy tows unprotected and struck at them spitefully

until, of the 22 whale tows that sailed from the Solent in fine weather, not one remained afloat.'

The full force of the gale hit Omaha Beach. Taylor continued:

> 'Breaches appeared rapidly in the breakwater. Blockships broke their backs and Phoenix caissons disintegrated, and through the breaks the sea struck at the roadways and the piers so that soon they were sinking. Then onto the half-submerged roadways drifting landing craft and equipment piled themselves, till an inextricably-jumbled mass of wreckage was torn from the moorings and cast upon the beaches, and along the edge of the sea a long length of whole roadway and wrecked craft trailed brokenly. The destruction was complete.'

Mulberry B, at first sight, seemed in no better condition. Taylor recalled that along the beach at Arromanches 'littered wreckage was piled high, casting itself near the high-water mark in a chaotic tangle of steel.' But despite appearances to the contrary, Mulberry B proved salvable, the full impact of the storm having been broken by the Calvados reef lying beyond the harbor. The remnants of the American Mulberry were towed east to repair the British harbor, and by the end of the month it was receiving 4000 tons of supplies each day.

LEFT: The Germans were to deploy some of their best divisions in an effort to crush the beachhead. Among the most infamous was the 12th SS Panzer Division 'Hitlerjugend,' whose present and future commander are seen here attending a meeting at Rommel's HQ on 17 June. From left to right: Brigadeführer Kurt 'Panzer' Meyer, Gruppenführer Fritz Witt, and Witt's aide-de-camp Hauptsturmführer Max Wünsche.

LEFT: The British failure to capture Caen on D-Day was to determine Montgomery's conduct of the battle. The ruined houses made excellent strong points from which teams like this one servicing an MG42 could inflict heavy casualties on the attacker. Thousands of French civilians also died in the ensuing battles.

LEFT: The British Armoured Vehicle Royal Engineers' (AVRE) 'Petard', seen here on the streets of Bayeux on 7 June was a most effective means of dealing with German strong points. The Petard was essentially a mortar which could hurl an explosive charge at a bunker at a very short range. Even the most strongly-constructed bunkers could seldom withstand more than a few direct hits.

Far more materiel, however, continued to be landed on open beaches. The problem which logisticians faced after the 'great storm' was not one of getting the supplies ashore, but of finding somewhere to store them in a beachhead.

The *Bocage*

The campaign was not going as planned. So much time had been spent on solving the problems of getting the troops and supplies ashore, that virtually no attention had been paid to the problems which troops might encounter once they were off the beaches. Allied troops had trained in large armored formations on Salisbury Plain, Dartmoor, Exmoor and the North Yorkshire Moors, preparing for the type of mobile warfare which had characterized operations in North Africa.

On the extreme left of the beachhead facing southeast, the British had established a small bridgehead across the Orne, overlooking country not unlike that of Salisbury Plain. However, the bridgehead was considered too small to allow armored divisions to concentrate there in any strength, and certainly not in secret. To the immediate west the situation was even worse. Here British troops faced the industrial suburbs of Caen, which the Germans had defended. All armies subscribed to an article of faith which prohibited armored divisions attacking defended cities.

A few miles to the west of Caen, and extending to the swamps and marshes of the Cotentin peninsula, lay the *bocage*, an intricate patchwork of sunken lanes and small fields bounded by ancient hedgerows: hedgerows over three meters thick at the base and rising to a height of more than five meters. Large farmhouses or small villages studded the land at intervals of roughly one kilometer. The farmhouses' thick-walled stone buildings with deep cellars were relics of the time five centuries earlier when Normandy had been a battleground in the closing phase of the Hundred Years War. To make matters worse, about 16 kilometers inland the country began to rise to a tangle of hills, the highest of which, 360-meter Mont Pinçon, lay at the center of an area the Normans called 'Normandie Suisse', because of its resemblance to the Alpine foothills.

The Normandy countryside was an aggressor's nightmare and a defender's paradise: an intricate network of natural and manmade obstacles, with thousands of strongly-built houses, many of which could withstand all but a direct hit from a heavy bomb or a large caliber shell.

Plans and Counterplans

At first neither the Allies nor the Germans had any intention of going on the defensive. For Montgomery, the imperative was to expand the beachhead. The terrain in which this could be done most effectively lay to the immediate east and west of Caen. Offensives in these areas accorded well with his pre-invasion plans, which were predicated on a British expansion to the southeast, designed to enable the Americans to strike northwest to Cherbourg, and southwest to the big port-cities of Brittany. After this initial phase, Montgomery had envisaged the Americans swinging east to catch up with the British, who would have reached the Seine.

For the Germans, just containing the beachhead was not enough. They knew that they had to crush it out of existence. For a time, von Rundstedt and Rommel remained convinced that the American landings were diversions: they therefore proposed to strike at the British to the east and west of Caen. On 9 June both the British and German high commands prepared offensives which were the mirror image of each other. Over the next 48 hours, to the east of Caen, the 21st Panzer and 346st Infantry Divisions attacking north ran into the 51st Highland Division and 4th Armoured Brigade which were preparing to attack south.

Meanwhile, to the west of Caen, the Panzer 'Lehr' and 12th SS 'Hitlerjugend' Panzer divisions ran into the Canadian 3rd Division and the bulk of British XXX Corps. In fact, the German drives barely got beyond their starting lines; the Panzer 'Lehr' Division managed to penetrate British positions quite deeply, but opened up a gap thereby between its left flank and the main German line. Sensing an opportunity for a breakout, Montgomery ordered XXX Corps' spearhead, the renowned 7th Armoured Division, to move due west along the coast almost to the American sector, and then swing due south-southeast through the gap, to Villers Bocage, a town straddling RN175, which ran eight miles northeast to Caen. 7th Armoured Division was, in effect, to encircle the Panzer 'Lehr' Division and attack Caen from the undefended south.

Villers Bocage

At first all went well. The advance guard of the 7th Armoured Division, the 4th County of London Yeomanry with a detachment of the Rifle Brigade, reached Villers Bocage on the morning of 13 June, then turned northeast up RN175, and drove for about a mile in single file along the narrow hedge-

RIGHT: The most effective tank the Allies possessed, the Sherman Firefly, mounting a 17-pounder gun. This was the only Allied tank capable of meeting the German Panther and Tiger on anything like equal terms. Unfortunately on 13 June 1944 7th Armoured Division's Fireflys were not attached to the 4th County of London Yeomanry when the regiment encountered Obersturmführer Wittmann.

lined road to a low hill, marked Point 213 on Allied maps. From here the commander of the lead vehicle could see the distant chimneys of Colombelles, the industrial suburb of Caen. A few hundred meters south of point 213, Obersturm-führer Michel Wittmann, peering through the vision slit of his heavily-camouflaged Tiger tank, could see the turrets of the British tanks above the hedgerows, stretching along the road like ducks in a shooting gallery. Wittmann fired, hit the tank on Point 213, and blocked the possibility of the British advancing; he fired again, hit a tank about 900 meters back toward Villers Bocage, and thus prevented the possibility of a British retreat. In the next five minutes Wittmann fired another 23 times, each shot destroying a British vehicle.

The crews of the Shermans and Cromwells swung their 75mm guns onto the Tiger, only to watch in horror as their shells bounced off the German tank's frontal armor. While Wittmann withdrew to take on more ammunition, three Panther tanks of Wittmann's company joined in the shooting and completed the massacre. In total, four German tanks destroyed 53 British tanks and other vehicles. The debacle of Villers Bocage effectively ended Montgomery's first attempt to break out to the west of Caen. It also demoralized 7th Armoured Division, and spread alarm and despondency throughout the Allied armies.

LEFT: Wittmann's victory at Villers Bocage severely affected the morale of 7th Armoured Division, many of whose personnel were entering their fifth year of war. The 11th Armoured Division, seen here passing through the village of Herouvillette on 14 June, had as yet to experience combat and were still enthusiastic. They too would soon learn to respect the Panzers.

BELOW LEFT: Even before the 'Great Storm', most supplies for the American First Army had to be landed over open beaches. This led to increasing congestion on the beachhead and the need to take Cherbourg as quickly as possible. But just inland from this scene the countryside changed dramatically, with half-tracks and trucks becoming a liability rather than an asset.

ABOVE RIGHT: Inland from Omaha and Utah the Americans plunged into the *bocage*. This was infantry combat at its most difficult, platoons fighting along narrow lanes and through dense hedgerows. This technique for locating enemy fire owed more to Hollywood films than to infantry training manuals, but was nevertheless effective.

RIGHT: The result of a skirmish near Carentan during the American drive across the Cotentin peninsula. A patrol of the 82nd Airborne Division has ambushed and annihilated a group of Germans. More often it was the Germans, fighting from concealed bunkers, who annihilated the Americans.

The Capture of Cherbourg

Meanwhile, in the American sector, Major General J Lawton Collins' VII Corps was inching its way forward, field by field, hedgerow by hedgerow, to capture the town of Carentan. Bradley then planned to drive due west to cut off the neck of the Cotentin peninsula, and then to exploit north to take Cherbourg from the landward side, and south to take Coutances and St Lô. The fighting here was very different from the tank-to-tank slogging matches experienced by the British around Caen: infantry platoons fought each other with machine guns and mortars from sunken lanes.

The Germans were heavily outnumbered, but put up a skillful resistance. By the time the 101st Airborne Division took Carentan on 12 June they had suffered very heavy casualties. Two days later the 82nd Airborne and 9th Infantry Divisions continued their advance to the west. The Germans fell back before them: Allied aircraft and Resistance attacks had severely depleted their stocks of ammunition. On 18 June VII Corps reached Burneville-sur-Mer, on the western coast of the Cotentin. Regrouping, Collins took the 4th, 9th and 29th Infantry Divisions north. By 20 June the Americans were fighting their way through the main German defense line: a

system of steel and concrete fortifications which lay in a 10 kilometer-long semicircle to the south of Cherbourg. Collins' troops would probably not have succeeded here had they been facing the Wehrmacht or the SS: however, most of the 25,000-strong garrison consisted of middle-aged administrative personnel, and over a fifth were units formed from Polish and Russian prisoners.

Massive air attacks on 22 June broke the morale of the defenders. Within 24 hours the three American divisions had penetrated the defense line in many places, and three days later the German commander surrendered. German engineers had already reduced the port to a shambles: sunken ships blocked the harbor, toppled cranes lay in a twisted mass of metal, and mines lay everywhere. It took another eight weeks to clear the wreckage, and until November before the port was brought back into full operation. The Germans had been customarily efficient; indeed, so thorough was the devastation that the Americans had to rely on supplies brought across open beaches.

Operation Epsom

While the Americans fought to secure Cherbourg, dramatic events had been taking place around Caen. Hitler flew to France on 17 June; after a conference with von Rundstedt and Rommel he became so alarmed by the despondency of his generals that he ordered two crack Panzer divisions to be transferred to Normandy from the Eastern Front. These forces, combined with those divisions already in Normandy, would give Rommel a significant, if temporary, qualitative superiority by the end of June. On 20 June Hitler ordered a

massive six-division strike towards Bayeux for 1 July; it would split the beachhead and would allow his forces to defeat the British and Americans comprehensively.

While the Führer was concocting his plans, Montgomery prepared for another break-out, this time much closer to Caen. Instead of trying to infiltrate an armored division through the *bocage*, this time Montgomery intended to launch the three divisions of VIII Corps in 'an all-out blitz attack' on 25 June, Derby Day – hence the codename for the offensive. The attack had two phases. At 0415 hours on 25 June the leading battalions of the 49th (West Riding) Division advanced through a thick morning mist toward the villages of Fontenay and Rauray, to secure a starting line for the second and main phase of the operation. The mist was so thick that it not only provided cover, but also served to break up the cohesion of the attacking units. By mid-morning the mist had cleared and German fire coming from the *bocage* to the southwest of Fontenay stopped the 49th Division.

At dawn on 26 June a tremendous barrage – more than 700 artillery pieces supplemented by naval guns – heralded the opening of the second phase. The 15th (Scottish), 43rd (Wessex) and 11th Armoured Divisions – a total of 60,000 men and 600 tanks – advanced on a narrow two-mile front east of Fontenay through the village of Cheux toward the River Odon. Once across, VIII Corps was to swing southeast of Caen and link up with the 51st Highland Division, which would be advancing southwest from the eastern side of Caen. VIII Corps' leading battalion, the Argyll and Sutherland Highlanders, stormed down to the river and seized an intact bridge at the village of Baron, over which the tanks of the 23rd

ABOVE LEFT: Within days of the landing the attrition rate in some American units was beginning to affect morale severely. The crack of a sniper's bullet was always a possibility, even when well behind the front line, as in this case near Carentan.

LEFT: The destruction of Cherbourg meant that the Americans would have to keep unloading supplies over open beaches. Thanks to the flat and sandy nature of the Cotentin coastline and the availability of flat-bottomed LSTs, this proved much less of a problem than many anticipated. These LSTs have come in on the flood tide and, as the water has receded, trucks have driven directly over the sand, as is indicated by the tire tracks. This form of 'roll-on roll-off' was probably more efficient than conventional unloading in a fully-equipped port.

ABOVE RIGHT: The beginning of Operation Epsom. Tanks of the 11th Armoured Division roll past a crashed fighter on their way to Cheux. From there they will drive south to the Odon.

RIGHT: Tanks of the East Riding Yeomanry supporting the attack of the 49th (West Riding) Division on Fontenay.

Hussars roared. During the next 48 hours the Hussars pushed on to take Hill 112, a 270-meter eminence dominating the southwestern approach to Caen. The Germans had been relying on their dual-purpose 88mm guns to hold the British tanks at bay, but constant attacks by Allied fighter-bombers cleared the way for the Hussars. One German survivor of the first battle for Hill 112 recalled:

'In the early afternoon came the end. About a dozen tanks were rolling toward us, when two formations of twin-engined Lightnings attacked. Where to fire first? At the planes or at the tanks? In the confusion of air attack, the tanks opened fire at us. Gun after gun was knocked out, and the crews with them. Only one thing to do – withdraw!'

On the afternoon of 28 June the British came very close to winning a major victory. The danger posed to the German position was all too apparent to Seventh Army commander, General Dollmann, who suffered a heart attack and died. In fact, the situation was far less serious than Dollmann had imagined. The Hussars on Hill 112 were very much alone: the

a corridor nearly 10 kilometers long and three kilometers wide, extending north from Hill 112. Advancing from the west were the 2nd, 9th, and 10th SS Panzer Divisions and Panzer 'Lehr', while from the east the 1st and 12th SS Panzer Divisions were heading, along with the battered, but still capable, 21st Panzer Division.

Four years earlier a situation like this would have spelled disaster for the British, but 1944 was not 1940. On the night of 29-30 June Dempsey ordered the Hussars back from Hill 112. The following morning the advancing Panzers were hit by massed artillery fire and broadsides from battleships and cruisers, while heavy bombers rained down high explosives. The bombers were not particularly discriminating. In an effort to block the advance of the 9th SS Panzer Division up RN 175, Lancasters reduced the town of Villers Bocage to a heap of smoldering rubble. It was a portent of things to come. Operation Epsom had failed – it was anything but the 'blitz attack' Montgomery had called for – but it had sucked in the divisions Hitler had allocated to the great German counter-offensive. The co-ordinated seven-division attack scheduled

vast bulk of the British forces were still north of the Odon. Too many tanks, trucks and men had been pushed south along too narrow a front. A massive traffic jam had developed in the streets of Cheux, a jam which stretched back to the starting line. Because the 49th Division had been unable to advance, the western flank of the jam was open, while small groups of 'Hitlerjugend' crawled through the wheat fields by Cheux sniping at the columns, adding to the confusion.

By the evening of 28 June, Dollmann's successor, Obergruppenführer Paul Hausser, who had commanded the formidable I SS Panzer Corps on the Eastern Front, had the situation firmly under control. Hausser ordered the Panzer divisions which had been assembling for the Bayeux offensive to head for Cheux. However, this was scarcely a well co-ordinated or rapid offensive action; Hausser feeding the divisions in piecemeal as they reached the Odon. By 29 June Ultra intercepters revealed to Montgomery just how precarious VIII Corp's position was becoming. The 15th and 43rd Infantry Divisions and the 11th Armoured Division occupied

for 1 July was the only hope the Germans had of splitting and then crushing the beachhead. Operation Epsom, although it did not succeed in its primary objective, disrupted and defeated the Germans' only real chance of an outright Normandy victory.

High Commands in Crisis

The first week of July saw both the British and the German high commands in crisis. On 2 July von Rundstedt called Field Marshal Wilhelm Keitel, Chief of OKW, with the news that the counteroffensive was over. When Keitel asked 'What shall we do?' an exasperated von Rundstedt exploded: 'Make peace, you fools!' Twenty-four hours later the Führer relieved von Rundstedt of his command, replacing him with Field Marshal Günther von Kluge, who was given instructions to hold the existing line, no matter what the cost.

Within the beachhead, Montgomery's position had become just as insecure as that of his erstwhile German counterpart. He tried to make the best of Operation Epsom,

ABOVE: With heavy-handed humor the Germans called the Sherman the 'Tommy Cooker'; the British, with their infinitely more macabre and subtle sense of the ridiculous, called this tank the 'Ronson' because in the words of a wartime advertizement 'it lights the first time.' Humor of this sort allowed the British to fight on after witnessing scenes like this — a Sherman hit by an 88mm round exploding into a sheet of flame during Operation Epsom.

LEFT: The Tiger was not invulnerable, though at times it must have seemed so. All tank crews detested fighting in built-up areas. Both these Panzers fell victim not to British tanks but to six and 17-pounder antitank guns firing from the protection of the ruined houses.

RIGHT: This Panzergrenadier of the 12th SS can barely be 16 years old, but his extreme youth made him and his comrades capable of acts of daring which older soldiers dismissed as foolhardy. In the battle for Caen these teenagers imposed heavy casualties on the Allies.

claiming that it was part of a grand strategic design to draw the bulk of the German forces to the British part of the front, in order to allow the Americans a free run in the west. Epsom had certainly had this effect, but no one at SHAEF, not least Eisenhower himself, believed Montgomery's claims. Eisenhower sought Churchill's support in sacking Montgomery. For a few days the latter's position hung in the balance, but on the evening of 6 July the CIGS Alan Brooke, in the course of a blazing row with Churchill, forced the Prime Minister to support Montgomery against Eisenhower's attacks. The immediate threat to Montgomery's position had passed, but he was not yet secure, by any means.

Operations Windsor and Charnwood
Against a background of mounting criticism and pressure, Montgomery launched a third major offensive. Windsor and Charnwood were complementary operations designed both to expand the beachhead and to take the northwestern part of Caen. On 4 July, in Operation Windsor, the Canadian 8th Infantry Brigade, spearheaded by the Fort Garry Horse, advanced onto the northern part of Carpiquet airfield, just to the west of Caen. Units of the 'Hitlerjugend' resisted vigorously from concrete emplacements on the edge of the airfield and, after 24 hours, the Canadian offensive became bogged down. Forty-eight hours later the main assault, Operation Charnwood, went in against Caen. No army likes house-to-house fighting, and Montgomery was determined not to have his men sucked into a mini-Stalingrad: the trick was to remove the houses. At 2200 hours on 7 July, 500 heavy bombers dropped 2500 tons of high explosive onto the city, which was still packed with French civilians. The result was devastating. Most of the center and north of Caen was reduced to rubble, at least 6000 French civilians (mostly women and children) were blown to pieces or died of their injuries, and many thousands more were badly maimed. The bombing did disrupt German supply lines, but had very little effect on the German defenses which lay north of the built-up area. The British and Canadians finally broke through by concentrating overwhelming force (three divisions) against the German defenders, who held on until 9 July, suffering 6000 casualties in bitter close-quarter fighting. Some German positions fought to the death, succumbing only to the liquid fire of the flame-throwers of the Crocodile tanks. Neither had the British casualties been light – about 3500 killed, wounded and missing. However, by evening the British and Canadians held the northwestern part of the city. The industrial suburb of Colombelles to the northeast, and the half of Caen which lay southeast of the Orne, were still in German hands.

Operation Jupiter
The fighting in Caen had barely died down when Montgomery launched his fourth offensive, Operation Jupiter: an attack by the 43rd (Wessex) Division against German positions on Hill 112 to the west of Caen. It was the start of a vicious attritional struggle which was to go on unremittingly for nearly two weeks. In the first 36 hours 43rd Division suffered 200 casualties in its attempt to gain footholds on the northern slopes. A German counterattack on 11 July almost pushed the British off, but one battalion, the 4th Somerset Light Infantry, clung on in the face of near-impossible odds. At 0100 hours on 12 July the battalion launched a counterattack, which immediately ran into heavy resistance. One British survivor, Corporal Douglas Proctor, graphically recalled the horror of that night's attack:

> 'The leading section commander was attempting to scramble through the barbed wire ... a single enemy bullet pierced his belly and as a result exploded a phosphorous grenade he carried in his webbing pouch. Struggling in desperation he became entangled in the barbed wire and hung there, a living, screaming, human beacon. His only

release from the fiery hell, as he must have known, was to plead for someone to shoot him as quickly and mercifully as possible.'

The attack virtually wiped out 4th Somerset Light Infantry: of the 36 men in Corporal Proctor's platoon who went into action, only nine remained. The battalion was pulled off Hill 112, only for another to take its place. And so it went on, day after day, for another two weeks.

The Battle of the Hedgerows
By the middle of July the fighting in the British and Canadian sectors had become bogged down; the situation in the American sector was no better. After the fall of Cherbourg, Bradley had turned all his forces south. On 3 July VIII Corps, under the command of Major General Troy H Middleton, struck down the western coast of the Cotentin peninsula toward Coutances. Simultaneously, Major General Charles H Corlett's XIX Corps attacked southeast of Carentan, along the Vire River toward St Lô. In the center Bradley placed VII Corps under Collins, who had Périers as his objective, a town halfway between Coutances and St Lô.

The Americans advanced on a very broad front (nearly 48 kilometers) through country which was the *bocage* at its worst. By 15 July the four divisions which comprised VIII Corps had advanced just 11 kilometers, at a cost of 10,000 casualties. For VII Corps the situation was even worse. On 4 July one of its divisions, the 83rd, succeeded in advancing just 180 meters, at a cost of 1400 casualties. XIX Corps made no better progress. On 7 July an attempt by the 3rd Armored and 30th Infantry Divisions to exploit a gap in the German defenses ended with elements of both divisions mistaking one another for the Germans, and engaging in furious combat. Both divisions called in USAAF fighter-bombers, which strafed both of them without discrimination. Casualties were heavy; by the time the divisions were disentangled, the Germans had plugged the gap.

On 11 July XIX Corps slogged forward again, with the 29th and 35th Divisions pushing directly for St Lô. After several days of aerial and artillery bombardment, and after suffering more than 2000 casualties, the divisions succeeded in taking two hills overlooking St Lô. Below them lay a wilderness of rubble. St Lô, an important road junction, had been bombed and shelled since D-Day; the once picturesque medieval town had been reduced to ruins, and more than 800 French civilians had died. The troops of the 29th Division thought

ABOVE: Troops of the US 29th Division in action near St Lô during mid-July.

RIGHT: The ubiquitous 25-pounder field gun in action during the battle for Hill 112. The eight guns of this particular battery fired 4000 rounds in just 15 hours on the first day of the battle, more than one round per gun every 30 seconds. The barrels glowed white-hot and had to be regularly doused with water.

LEFT: Shermans support the 43rd (Wessex) Division in its attack on Hill 112, 10 July 1944. By the end of this epic struggle the slopes and crest of Hill 112 looked like a moonscape.

this particular battle as good as over, but when the 2nd and 3rd Battalions of the 116th Regiment tried to break into the town, intense German shellfire cut them off from the rest of the division. The commander of 3rd Battalion, Major Thomas D Howie, tried to continue the advance, but was killed the moment he broke cover. The rest of the 116th attacked the town on the night of 17 July, linked up with the isolated battalions, and by mid-morning were fighting their way into the center of the town. That afternoon the regiment took the body of Major Howie, draped in an American flag, to the center of St Lô, and laid it before the bombed-out shell of a church – a poignant symbol of the death and destruction which the Americans had both endured and inflicted to take this little town. That night, morale in St Lô was very low. It was scarcely higher anywhere else among the Allied armies in Normandy. The campaign was entering its seventh week. Already the Allies had suffered 122,000 casualties, had devastated the once-peaceful province of Normandy, killing and maiming tens of thousands of French civilians, and a break-out seemed as far away as ever.

8

BREAK-OUT

Plans and Preparations

For the Allied high command the Normandy campaign reached its nadir in the second week of July. Montgomery had run out of ideas – a fact which he later tried hard to disguise. His only remaining strategy was to hammer away relentlessly at the Germans. The policy barely differed from the one advanced by Haig on the Western Front in World War I. The weapons might have changed, but Windsor, Charnwood and Jupiter were a rerun of the same grinding attritional struggles.

Bradley was not much more optimistic about the American front. At the present rate of advance, the war looked set to continue forever. But by 8 July, after several days' hard thought, he hit on a new approach. Bradley decided to abandon the advance across a broad front. Instead he would concentrate his forces for a rapierlike thrust: technically the same maneuver as the British advance at Epsom, but in practice very different. He planned to concentrate the bulk of First Army in the center of the Cotentin north of the St Lô-Périers road, a very straight Roman road, easily recognizable from the air. He marked out a 10 square kilometer rectangular area just to the south of the road which the US Eighth Air Force would bomb to oblivion. As soon as the bombing stopped,

two armored and a motorized division would make a dash for Coutances, 24 kilometers to the southwest. From here they would advance to Avranches. Once Avranches had fallen, Bradley's divisions would 'turn the corner' and push westwards into Brittany to seize her large Atlantic ports.

The break-out was codenamed 'Operation Cobra.' When Bradley unfolded his plans to Montgomery and Dempsey on 10 July, he met an enthusiastic response. Montgomery agreed to support Cobra with massive British and Canadian attacks to the east of Caen. Like the American operation, these attacks (codenamed 'Goodwood' and 'Atlantic') would be spearheaded by an enormous aerial bombardment. At the meeting Goodwood and Atlantic were scheduled for 17 July, Cobra for 18 July. But soon after Dempsey and possibly also Montgomery began to change their minds about the nature and extent of the operation. Dempsey began to speak of it as if it were to be the major Allied break-out – a view widely held at SHAEF. The picture became more complicated a few days later, when Bradley discovered that some of his divisions were running low on ammunition. Cobra would have to be delayed until supplies were replenished. In the event bad weather forced a further delay. The two operations thus came to be seen as quite separate.

LEFT: Generals need to be good actors and Patton and Montgomery were among the best. In reality, they had loathed each other since first meeting in North Africa nearly 18 months earlier. Bradley stands between them smiling; perhaps he appreciated the irony of the situation.

ABOVE RIGHT: The breakthrough offensives scheduled to begin on 17 July, Operations Goodwood and Cobra, were to depend on heavy carpet bombing from US Eighth Air Force B-17s and Liberators, and RAF Bomber Command's Lancasters and Halifaxes.

RIGHT: USAAF planners plot a bomb line on a map prior to a carpet-bombing operation. Accurate navigation and bomb aiming was essential but these operations invariably resulted in very heavy Allied ground casualties.

Operations Goodwood and Atlantic

When Dempsey surveyed the front for a start line he focused attention on the extreme eastern end of the beachhead. On 6 June British paratroopers had here secured a small enclave on the south side of the Orne, now held by the 51st Highland Division. For about 10 kilometers south of their front the land was flat and relatively open, until it rose almost imperceptibly to the Bourguébus Ridge. It was flanked to the east by the German-controlled industrial suburb of Colombelles, to the west by the Bois de Bavent, a low, wooded ridge. Compared to other areas, it seemed almost ideal – a natural corridor for an armored assault. The only real drawbacks it held as a launching point for an assault were those of size and access. The enclave was a mere 10 square kilometers in area, reached by only three bridges across the Canal de Caen, and three across the Orne. Chaos would ensue if traffic control broke down as it had during Operation Epsom.

At dawn on 18 July 1500 heavy bombers deposited 5000 tons of high explosive on Colombelles and the Bois de Bavent. Shortly afterward, medium bombers dropped 2500 tons of fragmentation bombs down the corridor as far south as the Bourguébus Ridge. As the bombers departed, 1000 artillery pieces and heavy naval guns began a rolling bombardment. Behind this, the Canadian 3rd Division attacked into the rubble of Colombelles, while the British 3rd Division advanced into the Bois de Bavent. The tanks of the 11th Armoured Division rolled down the corridor as planned, followed by the Guards Armoured Division and the 7th Armoured Division; a total of 750 tanks, the largest armored offensive in British history. The only Germans they met were a pathetic handful, stupefied by the bombing, who wandered around aimlessly staring into space. Goodwood might have been successful if this momentum could have been sus-

tained. However, massive traffic jams were already building up within the enclave. The assault involved moving not only tanks, but a further 9000 vehicles across the Canal de Caen and the Orne. Instead of a remorseless armored torrent, tanks and trucks emerged in dribs and drabs. By mid-morning, 11th Armoured's tanks were straggling in long columns toward Bourguébus, their accompanying infantry left several miles north to deal with small pockets of resistance.

The Germans had picked up a clear picture of British plans some days earlier, thanks to radio interception and direct observation from the Colombelles' chimneys. Rommel could see that the British were planning a major offensive. He responded by ordering additional forces to deploy to a depth of more than 16 kilometers from the British front line. He also positioned the powerful 1st SS Panzer Division ('Leibstandarte Adolf Hitler') in woods on the southern slopes of the Bourguébus Ridge. Rommel had personally inspected these deployments on 17 July, and was well pleased: he had converted what appeared to be one of the weakest sectors of the German front into one of the strongest. Rommel missed the battle: driving back from his tour of inspection on the evening of 17 July, his staff car was strafed by British fighter-bombers. Rommel, badly injured and unconscious, was invalided back to Germany.

German preparations had been so thorough that Rommel's absence did not really matter. By mid-morning of 18 July, the advance guard of the 11th Armoured Division, the Fife and Forfar Yeomanry, was about six kilometers south of the start line, passing the heavily-bombed and apparently deserted village of Cagny. Suddenly all hell broke loose. German 88mm guns opened up from an orchard north of the village, hit the Fife and Forfar in its left flank, and within minutes effectively annihilated the regiment. At virtually the same

LEFT: Montgomery on 17 July, the day before Goodwood. An important part of Montgomery's role was maintaining the morale of his troops. Having left the detailed planning of the operation to the commander of the British Second Army, Lieutenant General Sir Miles Dempsey and VIII Corps' commander, Lieutenant General Sir Richard O'Connor, Montgomery visited the 50th Infantry Division to award medals for gallantry.

RIGHT: To compensate for the enormous Allied superiority in air power and artillery, the Germans constructed elaborate defense systems on the Normandy front. A company of the 12th SS Panzer Division ensconced in these bunkers kept an entire Canadian brigade at bay for more than a day at Carpiquet airfield to the west of Caen on 6 July. The Goodwood defenses were not as sophisticated, but even so most Germans survived the massive aerial and artillery bombardment.

LEFT: As the last of the B-17s disgorged its load around midday on 25 July, American artillery took over the support of the Cobra offensive. The guns put down one of the heaviest barrages in American military history.

RIGHT: Until the attachment of spikes to the front of the Shermans, these hedgerows presented major difficulties to the movement of armor and infantry. Equipped with spikes, a tank has ripped a wide path through the hedge, through which the infantry now advances.

time other British tanks to the southeast ran into the Panthers of the 1st SS Division, which had been completely untouched by the bombing, having sheltered on the southern slopes of the Bourguébus Ridge. Without infantry to attack the '88's, and heavily outranged by the Panthers, the 11th Armoured Division took huge casualties. The Guards Armoured Division, moving up to support, became hopelessly entangled with the rear elements of the 11th Armoured Division. The confusion was heightened by the sudden appearance of German tank-destroying teams armed with their version of the bazooka – the much more powerful 'Panzerschreck'. When the commander of the Guards Armoured Division, Major General Adair, saw a Panzerschreck team heading straight for him, he had to break off trying to sort out the situation, and order his driver to reverse at high speed; 7th Armoured Division now ran into the back of the Guards, and all cohesion disappeared. Many British tanks fought on, but as individual units. As the Panthers closed for the kill, the commander of 11th Armoured Division, Major General 'Pip' Roberts, finally managed to make radio contact with a 'cab rank' of Typhoon fighter-bombers. He directed them onto the Panthers coming over the Bourguébus Ridge, and then it was the turn of the Germans to take heavy casualties. British and German tanks continued to slog it out for another two days, until torrential rain on the night of 20 July turned the ground into a quagmire, making further movement impossible. The operation had not been a total Allied disaster: the Canadians had captured the rest of Caen, and the British, at a cost of 5500 casualties and 430 tanks (more than one-third of the total they had in Normandy) had managed to advance nearly 10 kilometers and take Bourguébus Ridge.

Crisis for Montgomery

Eisenhower and his staff at SHAEF accused Montgomery of failing to deliver the long-awaited break-out. Montgomery protested that he had made no such claims for Goodwood, but his protests fell on deaf ears. Air Chief Marshal Sir Trafford Leigh-Mallory summed up the mood at Eisenhower's headquarters with an incredulous 'Seven miles for seven thousand tons of bombs!' Eisenhower again moved for Montgomery's dismissal and ominously, on 20 July, Churchill flew to Montgomery's headquarters. But Montgomery had always been a lucky general. Shortly before he was due to receive Churchill, he was brought the electrifying news of the attempted assassination of Hitler and an apparent coup in Berlin. Churchill was dumbfounded; whatever else might have been on his mind quickly paled into insignificance. He left Montgomery in very high spirits, clutching a gift from the general – a bottle of excellent French brandy. Later that day Eisenhower visited Montgomery. The meeting was strained, but Eisenhower left satisfied that even if it had not been Montgomery's intention, the Goodwood offensive had ensured that virtually all the German armored forces were now concentrated on the British front. If Bradley's divisions could now break out from the *bocage* and get to the open country beyond Coutances, there was very little the Germans could do to stop them.

Operation Cobra

Ever since they had first plunged into the *bocage*, American tank crews had been trying to find ways of moving across country without their tanks 'bellying up' over hedges. A tank stuck at an angle of 45 degrees in the air was useless and vulnerable. The crew could not bring its guns to bear, while its lightly-armored bottom was exposed to antitank fire. Hundreds of Shermans had been lost in this way. Crews had experimented with a variety of cutting devices to allow a tank to go through, rather than over, a hedge, but all had failed, until an NCO in the 102nd Cavalry Reconnaissance Squadron, Sergeant Curtis G Culin Jr, welded a row of spikes to the front of his tank. It was a brilliant and simple solution. The spikes dug into the bottom of the hedge, preventing the tank 'bellying' and, by going forward and then reversing, the tank behaved like a gigantic garden fork, literally uprooting the hedge. By the last week of July, about three-fifths of all American tanks had been equipped with Culin's spikes. So far none had been employed in combat: Bradley had decided to keep them as a surprise until Cobra was underway.

The offensive opened badly. Heavy rain had led to Cobra's postponement until 24 July, but on that day the sky was still overcast. At the last moment Bradley decided to delay for another 24 hours, but some of the squadrons tasked with the opening bombardment did not receive his signal. About 300 flew on, and in poor visibility dropped 700 tons of bombs, some of which landed on the Americans, killing and wound-

ing 126. At 1100 hours the following morning the bombers returned, this time dropping 3300 tons of high explosive. Even more landed on American positions, killing and wounding another 600. Among the dead was Lieutenant General Lesley J McNair, the highest-ranking American officer killed during World War II, who had been in Normandy on a fact-finding tour for the Joint Chiefs of Staff in Washington.

Though many of the American front-line units were stunned and dazed, the attack went ahead. They advanced behind a massive rolling artillery barrage only to discover that their opponents, the grenadiers of Panzer 'Lehr', were as formidable as ever. On the first day progress was painfully slow. On 26 July it seemed to get easier. Equipped with their *bocage*-tearing spikes, Shermans were able to move around positions which would once have held them up for days, and to hit them from the rear or from the flanks. On 27 July there was no mistake: despite the difficulties of the terrain, the momentum of the American advance was picking up. On 28 July the Americans knew that they were winning. The country was beginning to open up and drivers could now get their tanks out of low gear. Late that evening the advance guard of VIII Corps rolled into Coutances.

After 52 days of grinding attritional struggle, the Americans had ripped through the extreme western end of the German line. It was now that they reaped the benefits of the British Army's slogging matches: the Germans had nothing left to stop them. On 29 July they raced the 24 kilometers to Avranches, and on 30 July crossed the Sélune river into Brittany. The Germans now suffered another blow. Even at the end of July, the German high command had still believed that a substantial American army under General Patton was stationed in eastern England, waiting to descend on the Pas de Calais. Anticipating an attack, they kept substantial forces northeast of the Seine. On 1 August the nightmare became reality, but Patton's army, the newly-formed Third, did not oblige the Germans by attacking across the straits of Dover. Instead it surged through the gap at Avranches on the German's broken left flank.

Patton's Charge

During the next five days Patton's tank columns tore over northwestern France. Third Army's 4th Armored Division raced across Brittany to Lorient, 6th Armored Division was outside Brest by 6 August, while the 83rd Infantry Division closed on St Malo. Meanwhile, on 5 August, Third Army's XV Corps, under Major General Wade H Haislip, emerged from the Avranches gap and struck southeast. By 9 August XV Corps' advance guard had reached Le Mans, 136 kilometers southeast of Avranches. One hundred and ninety kilometers to the west lay the Seine; 95 kilometers to the north lay the British and Canadian front at Caen.

ABOVE LEFT: Mail call for some GIs of US VIII Corps on 27 July 1944. Unshaven, dirty, disheveled and grinning, these men know that they are winning.

LEFT: On 1 August 1944 came the moment Patton had been waiting for. His tank columns burst through the Avranches gap into the German rear areas, Patton was invariably close to the most advanced units.

ABOVE: While the armor made glamorous advances, the infantry was left to secure the towns.

RIGHT: By 1 August American vehicles clogged the roads for kilometers north of Avranches, as they sought to clear the traffic jams and exploit west and south. Congestion on this scale was possible only because fighters like these North American P-51 Mustangs had made it too dangerous for the Luftwaffe to fly by day.

Operations Spring and Bluecoat

While the Americans were making their spectacular break-through, the Canadians and British kept up the pressure. On 25 July the Canadian II Corps launched Operation Spring, an assault south of Caen toward the small towns of May-sur-Orne, Verrières and Tilly-la-Compagne, designed to ensure that the Germans could not move any divisions westward. Unknown to the Canadians, the Germans had ensconced themselves securely within this area in the deep shafts and lateral tunnels of a complex of iron mines. Here they had complete protection from air and artillery bombardment, and could move substantial forces through the tunnels to any area of the front which was threatened. This was the strongest German position in Normandy; on 25 July alone the Canadians suffered 1500 casualties, of whom nearly one-third were killed. It was their worst day of the war, with the single exception of Dieppe. Gains were negligible.

As the Canadian attack faltered, Montgomery received an urgent message from Brooke. Eisenhower had again been complaining to Churchill about the apparent inability of the British to advance, and Brooke warned that the Army 'must attack at the *earliest possible moment.*' This was a tall order. Three-quarters of the German armor was still concentrated against the British. As Montgomery wrote to Dempsey, another Allied attack in the area of Caen 'was unlikely to succeed.' Scanning the map of the front, the British commanders agreed that the only prospect for success lay in moving the whole of XXX and VIII Corps about 30 kilometers west of Caen, almost to the British boundary with the Americans, where Ultra intercepters indicated that there were no German armored formations.

Dempsey launched this operation, codenamed 'Bluecoat,' on 30 July. Advancing south along the boundary with the Americans, 11th Armoured Division, the spearhead of VIII Corps, smashed into and defeated a battlegroup of the 21st Panzer Division, and came to within three kilometers of the town of Vire, only 40 kilometers east of Avranches. Both Dempsey and Montgomery sensed that a major British victory was in the offing – all VIII Corps now had to do was to drive due west to Avranches, thereby trapping the still-substantial German forces south of St Lô. Unfortunately all was not well on VIII Corp's eastern flank. XXX Corps should have advanced in tandem with VIII Corps, but the heavily-defended Mont Pinçon lay directly to the south. It was scarcely surprising that after some minor gains, XXX Corps' attack became bogged down, leaving the whole of VIII Corps' eastern flank exposed to German counterattack. Alerted by Ultra that two Panzer divisions were indeed moving west, Dempsey decided he could not afford to take a risk and halted VIII Corps' advance. Montgomery felt that XXX Corps' failure to advance had cheated him out of a victory which would have matched that of El Alamein. On 3 August he sacked the commanders of both XXX Corps, and XXX Corps' most famous formation, 7th Armoured Division. But the real problem lay not with the commanders, but with the soldiers themselves, who were now in their fifth year of war.

The Mortain Counterattack

Even though Bluecoat had failed, Allied high command fully expected that the Germans in Normandy, mindful of the rapid American advance eastward from Avranches, would soon begin to withdraw towards the Seine to form a new

ABOVE: A battery of six-pounder antitank guns is towed toward Vire to support VIII Corps' advance on 1 August 1944. For a while it seemed that Operation Bluecoat was going to produce a spectacular British victory.

LEFT: Troops of XXX Corps advancing cautiously through the *bocage* on the lower slopes of Mont Pinçon on 1 August 1944. The Germans had laced the area with mines, one of which has detonated under this half-track.

RIGHT: XXX Corps was having a hard time of it on Mont Pinçon. A Sherman of the 7th Armoured Division rolls forward to deal with a machine-gun post which has held up British infantry.

RIGHT: In order to delay and channel Allied attacks, the Germans laid dense minefields along virtually every road and track. Clearing the mines by hand was a dangerous and time-consuming business. Flail tanks like this literally beat the ground, detonating the mines. The explosion of an antipersonnel mine caused little damage, but when an antitank mine went off, the chains and the drum usually needed to be replaced.

defense line. This was exactly what many German commanders planned to do. However, over 2000 kilometers east, in the Wolf's Lair in East Prussia, Adolf Hitler was convinced that his forces were on the verge of a major victory. Hitler, having survived the 20 July assassination attempt, was now convinced that the numerous disasters which had befallen his forces since 1942 were the work of treacherous anti-Nazi generals. Now that the Gestapo was weeding them out, the scene was set for a return to the spectacular victories of 1940 and 1941. Poring over the map of Normandy, it was obvious to the Führer that Avranches was the key to the American advance – every item of equipment to sustain Patton's divisions had to pass through that town, and the American-controlled corridor around Avranches was only 24 kilometers wide.

Having been promised early-morning fog by meteorologists, on the night of 6-7 August four Panzer divisions advanced from Mortain to Avranches, just 32 kilometers to the northwest. That first night the Panzers penetrated 11 kilometers into American lines, and cut off some American battalions. For a short time it seemed that Hitler's gambling instinct might indeed pay off. But as dawn broke, there was not a cloud in the sky. By mid-morning the sky over Avranches was filled instead with Allied fighter-bombers, forcing the Germans to go to ground during the hours of daylight. For the next 72 hours the Germans lay hidden by day, and attacked by night.

Eisenhower flew to Bradley's headquarters for a crisis meeting on 7 August; the American commanders decided to keep pushing divisions through the Avranches gap, come what may. If the Germans succeeded in plugging the gap and cutting off the American Third Army, Eisenhower personally guaranteed airdrops of 2000 tons per day to Patton's divisions. To Bradley and Eisenhower the Mortain counterattack seemed like a gift from the gods of war. The Germans, by ignoring Patton's surge to the east, and pumping more and

more men and machines westward toward Avranches, were helping to create the very conditions by which a large part of their army in northern France could be encircled. On 8 August, when the eastern spearhead of Patton's Third Army, Haislip's XV Corps, reached Le Mans, Bradley ordered it to turn north and head via Alençon and Argentan for the British sector of the Normandy beachhead. Now all Bradley had to do was to convince the British to strike south toward Argentan, and meet up with the Americans.

Operation Totalize

Quite independently of Eisenhower, Bradley or, for that matter, Montgomery, Lieutenant General Simmonds, the commander of the Canadian II Corps, had planned to attack south from Caen to Falaise on 8 August. This was the 26th anniversary of the great Canadian assault on the German Army during the Battle of Amiens in World War I. This assault had contributed greatly to breaking the morale of the Imperial German Army, and had ushered in the German collapse. Simmonds was hoping history would repeat itself. The experience of numerous disappointing failures had hardened the Canadians' determination to succeed. After dusk on 8 August, 1000 heavy bombers blasted the flanks of the corridor leading down to Falaise; the corridor itself was untouched. With no preliminary bombardment, two columns of tanks rolled forward, and with them went infantry in 'Kangaroos', tanks from which the turrets had been removed. At long last the Allies had an armored personnel carrier! The surprise was complete. By dawn the Canadian columns, now joined by Major General S Maczek's recently-landed 1st Polish Armored Division, were pushing toward Falaise.

The Germans counterattacked at 1130 hours. In one of the most extraordinary tank battles of all time, Michel Wittmann drove his lone Tiger at a squadron of Shermans, only to find that instead of reversing they came straight for him; he had had the misfortune to run into part of the Polish Armored

LEFT: Shortly after the assassination attempt of 20 July, Hitler took Mussolini to visit the briefing room in the Wolf's Lair. Far from shaking his confidence, the attempt on his life allowed Hitler to rationalize German defeats since 1942 as the work of treacherous Prussian generals.

RIGHT: An indication of the price which all armies were paying in the Normandy campaign: Allied casualties being shipped back to England and hospital on 15 August. On the day this picture was taken thousands of Germans were in a similar condition within the Falaise pocket, but there were to be no comfortable beds for them.

Division. Wittmann destroyed many of the Polish tanks, but still they kept advancing. Some got around his flanks, and five Shermans, coming up behind him, fired volleys at point-blank range, which blew Wittmann and his Tiger to pieces. The Canadians and Poles beat off the German counteroffensive, and at 1400 hours prepared to resume the attack. Five hundred B-17s flew overhead to pulverize the Germans, but ended up by repeating the Cobra disaster. Many bombs dropped short, more than 300 Canadians and Poles were killed and wounded, and many tanks were destroyed. The attack had got off to a bad start. The following day a Canadian battlegroup, the 28th Armored Regiment and the Algonquin Regiment, became hopelessly lost in the advance. It ran into two German Panzer groups and was fired on simultaneously by the Polish 1st Armored Division. Caught between the Germans and the Poles the Canadians were annihilated.

Operation Tractable

Totalize would have petered out but for the extraordinary situation developing to the south, where the Americans were pushing toward Argentan. It was imperative for some of the British forces to get to Falaise. During the next four days a revitalized Totalize, renamed 'Tractable', was put together. Totalize had relied on innovation and surprise; Tractable was an all-out onslaught. Massed artillery put down a creeping barrage, part high explosive and part smoke, to mask movement. Behind the wall of explosives came 300 tanks and four brigades of infantry, riding with the tanks in Kangaroos. Above, nearly 800 Lancasters and Halifaxes flew toward German positions.

Then everything went wrong. Once again many of the bombers dropped short of their target, killing and wounding more than 400 Canadians and Poles. Ignoring the casualties, the armored columns pressed forward, but in the dense clouds of smoke they soon lost their cohesion and collided with each other. Now in total disarray, the Shermans and

Kangaroos rolled down to a stream, the Laison, which ran across the line of advance but which had been considered too small to worry about. It may have been small (four meters wide) but its banks were steep – a natural antitank ditch. The armored columns were left milling round in confusion on the north side. Eventually fascine-carrying AVREs managed to bridge the Laison at several points. The tanks continued to advance, but the dash had become a crawl. On 15 August the Canadians finally entered Falaise. It had taken a week to cover 22 kilometers. During this time the Americans had advanced nearly 100 kilometers north of Le Mans, and were now at Argentan, less than 30 kilometers to the south.

The Falaise Pocket

Hitler still believed that armored counterstrokes would bring Germany victory. He ordered Field Marshal von Kluge to maintain pressure at Avranches, and to strike simultaneously at Falaise and Argentan to prevent the Canadian and American jaws meeting. On 15 August von Kluge made a tour of inspection of forces, inside what was clearly now a pocket. Like Rommel, he was strafed by fighter-bombers and barely made it out alive. That evening he informed Berlin 'No matter how many orders are issued, the troops cannot, are not able to, are not strong enough, to defeat the enemy. It would be a fateful error to succumb to a hope that cannot be fulfilled.' Without waiting for Hitler's reply, von Kluge ordered the troops to begin withdrawing from the pocket. In a rage Hitler dismissed von Kluge, ordered him back to Germany (the hapless von Kluge took cyanide rather than return) and, on 17 August, replaced him with Field Marshal Walther Model, a dedicated Nazi fresh from the Eastern Front. Model had survived many difficult situations in Russia, and he quickly realized that there was nothing to do other than to continue the withdrawal, while striking at Falaise and Argentan with any armor he could lay his hands on in order to keep the jaws open for as long as possible.

LEFT: On 13 August Patton was with advance units on the outskirts of Argentan when Bradley ordered him to stop. His threat to keep on going and 'drive the British into the sea' was clearly made in a moment of extreme frustration and annoyance, sentiments clearly reflected in his gaze.

BELOW: By 15 August the Germans were hitting back violently in a last desperate effort to keep the Falaise pocket from collapsing. Some of the worst street fighting took place in Domfront, pictured here, on the southwestern flank of the pocket.

RIGHT: Light reconnaissance vehicles like these US examples were sufficiently fast and agile to operate in daylight.

LEFT: By 19 August the Falaise pocket was beginning to collapse. Here an American patrol moves past a knocked-out Panzer IV in the ruins of Argentan.

BELOW: On the same day the Argyll and Sutherland Highlanders rounded up prisoners on the northern side of the pocket, the event recorded by the cine-cameraman to the left. Note the German officer: despite the privations of the pocket, he has shaved, his uniform is relatively clean, and he is clearly still in command.

By 19 August the German situation was desperate. The Polish 1st Armored Division had advanced southeast, and a Polish battlegroup of 1800 men and 80 tanks held the ridge of Mont Ormel in the middle of the corridor. From here they directed artillery fire and airstrikes against the German columns retreating on either side of the ridge. Oberfeldwebel Hans Erich Braun, one of the survivors of the 2nd Panzer Division, was on the receiving end. He remembered the withdrawal as a passage through the circles of hell:

'The never-ending detonations – soldiers waving to us,

begging for help – the dead, their faces screwed up still in agony – huddled everywhere in trenches and shelters, the officers and men who had lost their nerve – burning vehicles from which piercing screams could be heard – a soldier stumbling, holding back the intestines which were oozing from his abdomen – soldiers lying in their own blood – arms and legs torn off – others, driven crazy, crying, shouting, swearing, laughing hysterically – and the horses, some still harnessed to the shafts of their ruined wagons, appearing and disappearing in clouds of smoke

LEFT: It is often forgotten that the Allied forces had multibarreled rocket launchers. During the crushing of the Falaise pocket these weapons sent high-explosive rockets into German columns.

RIGHT: Debris in the Falaise pocket, 21 August 1944. The entire area of the pocket was like this: kilometer after kilometer of wrecked and abandoned equipment.

BELOW: While artillery, both conventional and rocket, was responsible for considerable damage within the pocket, the most devastating attacks had come from the air. Commandos relax in the sun while ground crews attach bombs to the belly of a RAF fighter-bomber at an airfield in Normandy.

and dust like ghosts — and the horses, again, screaming terribly, trying to escape the slaughter on the stumps of their hind legs.'

Taking reserves from outside the pocket, Model sent two Panzer divisions against Mont Ormel. Even though they were heavily outnumbered, the Poles fought back, their morale sky-high. Their radios were tuned to the BBC, which broadcast regular reports from Warsaw where the Polish Home

Army had risen against the Germans. Apart from on the streets of Warsaw, there was nowhere else that these Poles would have preferred to be; the Germans were everywhere, and the Poles were killing them in large numbers. At that very moment, 32 kilometers south, Major General Jacques Philippe Leclerc's recently-landed French 2nd Armored Division was attacking north from Argentan. The French, too, had another battle on their minds. On Saturday 19 August

Paris, like Warsaw, had risen in insurrection. Leclerc's men fought at Argentan until, on 21 August, the jaws snapped shut, and the encirclement was complete. Twenty-four hours later, the columns of the French 2nd Armored Division were racing for their capital. The battle for Normandy was over.

During the 11 weeks of fighting very little had gone according to plan, either for the Allies or the Germans. The Allies had expected huge casualties on the first day; instead, with

ABOVE: Frustrated by the halt at Argentan, on 19 August Patton had sent two divisions across the Seine south of Paris. Here the river was relatively narrow, and the crossing was made without difficulty. A week later the British 43rd (Wessex)

Division carried out an assault crossing of the formidable lower Seine at Vernon. This photograph, taken two days later (28 August,) shows 43rd Division's Bren-gun carriers crossing the newly-completed pontoon bridge.

the exception of the Omaha debacle, casualties had been lighter than anticipated. The Germans, expecting a landing in the Pas de Calais, continued to believe until late July that Normandy was a diversion, albeit a very powerful one. They had therefore failed to concentrate sufficient force quickly enough to crush the beachhead when it was in its infancy. For their part, the Allies had anticipated a quick advance off the beaches, and the development of maneuver warfare through-

out northern France, in which their massive numerical superiority in armor and aircraft would give them a decided advantage. The Germans were not strong enough to crush the beachhead, and for many weeks the Allies were not strong enough to break out.

The form of warfare which developed was very much like that of the Western Front in World War I. Generals who had gained their reputations in the rapid armored thrusts and counterstrokes of North African deserts or the Russian Steppes found themselves fighting battles remarkably similar to those waged by Haig and Ludendorff. Again and again the Allies launched set-piece offensives, supported by massed artillery fire and aerial bombardment, for very modest gains. Again and again the Germans were able to resist from heavily-fortified and ingeniously-camouflaged positions, redeploying their largely horsedrawn artillery and their largely non-mechanized and nonmotorized infantry by night to those

LEFT: On 23 August General Leclerc's Free French 2nd Armored Division and the US 4th Infantry Division moved southeast from Argentan toward Paris. Forty-eight hours later Leclerc had entered the city and reached the Arc de Triomphe.

BELOW: The liberation of Paris was not without bloodshed. On 25 August there was heavy fighting between units of Leclerc's division and elements of the German garrison in the south of the city.

LEFT: German snipers were active in central Paris. Here, the Free French 2nd Armored Division troops, assisted enthusiastically but probably inaccurately by members of the Resistance, return German fire.

BELOW: A tense moment for part of the German garrison holding out in the Chamber of Deputies on 25 August. A German officer who has just negotiated a surrender with the Resistance, attempts to convince his terrified men that they will be treated as prisoners of war and will not be shot out of hand.

areas of their line in which a breakthrough was threatened. The result was static, attritional warfare: the side with the most men and materiel would eventually win. The casualties reflected the nature of the fighting: between 6 June and 22 August the Allies lost 200,000, the Germans 400,000, and the French (both Resistance and civilians) about 100,000 – a total of some 700,000 men in 77 days. The Battle of the Somme, one of the greatest blood baths of World War I, lasted 141 days and cost the British, French and Germans 1,250,000 casualties. This comparison is crude, but serves to underline the fact that the fighting in Normandy was every bit as dreadful as the fighting on the Western Front during World War I.

The staff at SHAEF, from Eisenhower down, became bitterly critical of Montgomery for his failure to produce a breakthrough, but it is difficult to see how else he could have conducted the campaign. Likewise, virtually every German general criticized Hitler's insistence that the line be held.

Once the Americans broke the German line at the beginning of August, the impossibility of the Germans matching the Allies in maneuver warfare rapidly became apparent: Leclerc's troops reached Paris on 25 August, Patton's Third Army reached Verdun on 31 August, Hodges' First Army was in Mons on 2 September, and a day later Dempsey's Second Army liberated Brussels. As the war entered its sixth year there were many in the Allied nations who believed that it would 'all be over by Christmas.' This optimism was as misplaced as the earlier expectation that once the Allied armies were safely ashore the Germans would be quickly out-maneuvered and outfought. There was to be no cheap and easy victory. Ahead lay another winter of grinding attrition.

ABOVE: GIs of the US 4th Division entering Paris on 25 August, surrounded by a growing crowd of cheering Parisians, many of whom are attractive young women. Fifty years on, surviving GIs remembered this as one of the finest days of their lives.

RIGHT: The Champs Elysées, 26 August 1944, with De Gaulle to the fore. Many felt that this was the day on which the war should have ended. Unfortunately the Germans still had some nasty surprises in store.

INDEX

Figures in *italics* refer to illustrations

ACKNOWLEDGMENTS

The publisher would like to thank D23 for designing this book, Clare Haworth-Maden for editing it, Suzanne O'Farrell for the picture research, and Pat Coward for compiling the index.

The following individuals and agencies provided the illustrations:

Brompton Books, pages: 4-5 (Navy Department/US National Archives), 7 (both), 8 (top/National Archives of Canada), 8 (bottom), 10-11 (all three), 12 (top), 14, 21 (top/US Army), 24, 26 (bottom/US Army), 28 (US Army), 29 (top/US Army), 31 (top/US Army), 34 (Navy Department/US National Archives), 46 (bottom/Navy Department/US National Archives), 48 (all three/US Department of Defense), 50 (Navy Department/US National Archives), 54 (National Archives of Canada), 59, 70 (bottom/Navy Department/US National Archives), 74 (top), 77 (bottom/US Army), 78 (bottom/Navy Department/US National Archives), 84 (US Army), 85 (both), 87 (National Archives of Canada), 89 (US Army), 90 (top/US Army), 90 (bottom), 91 (top/US Army), 91 (bottom), 98 (US Army), 99 (both), 100 (US Army), 101 (National Archives of Canada), 102, 110.
Bundesarchiv, pages: 12 (bottom), 13 (top), 74 (center), 80, 81 (bottom), 96.
Imperial War Museum, London, pages: 1, 16, 17 (bottom), 21 (bottom), 23

(both), 30, 31 (bottom), 41 (top), 42 (top), 55 (bottom), 56 (top), 62, 66-67, 74 (bottom), 76 (top), 79 (both), 86, 103 (both), 104-105.
Keystone, Paris, page: 17 (top).
TRH, pages: 2-3 (US Department of Defense), 9, 13 (bottom), 25 (US Army), 32-33 (all three/US Department of Defense), 35 (top/US Navy), 36-37 (all three/US Department of Defense), 39 (both/US Army), 41 (bottom/US Department of Defense), 42 (bottom/US Department of Defense), 45 (US Army), 47 (bottom/US Army), 51 (top/US Coastguard), 51 (bottom/US Department of Defense), 52 (US Army), 53 (top and bottom/Imperial War Museum), 56 (center and bottom/Imperial War Museum), 57 (all three/Imperial War Museum), 58 (Imperial War Museum), 70 (top/Imperial War Museum), 71 (top/US Coastguard), 71 (center/US Army), 71 (bottom/US Navy), 92 (Imperial War Museum), 93 (bottom/Imperial War Museum).
Photothèque Plon-Perrin, pages: 6, 18 (top), 19 (both), 40, 64, 65 (bottom), 68-69, 77 (top), 106.
Hulton Deutsch, pages: 15, 22, 26 (top), 27, 29 (bottom), 35 (bottom), 38, 46 (top), 47 (top), 49 (both), 53 (center), 55 (top), 60 (center), 63 (top), 76 (bottom), 78 (top), 81 (top), 82, 83 (both), 88, 93 (top), 94-95, 97, 107, 108, 109, 110.
SIRPA/ECPA FRANCE, pages: 60 (top and bottom), 61, 63 (bottom).
COLLECTION VIOLLET, pages: 65 (top), 66, 68.